How to Build ALTERED WHEELBASE Cars

Steve Magnante

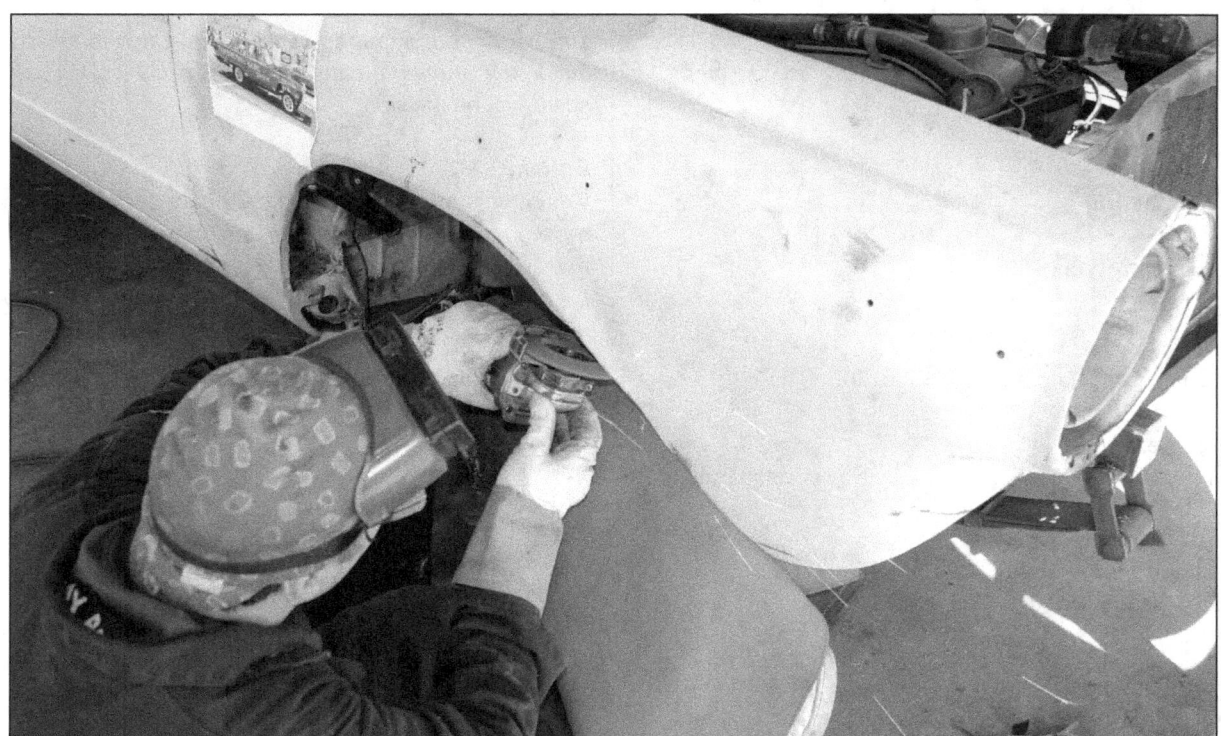

CarTech®

CarTech®
CarTech®, Inc.
39966 Grand Avenue
North Branch, MN 55056
Phone: 651-277-1200 or 800-551-4754
Fax: 651-277-1203
www.cartechbooks.com

© 2010 by Steve Magnante

All rights reserved. No part of this publication may be reproduced or utilized in any form or by any means, electronic or mechanical, including photocopying, recording, or by any information storage and retrieval system, without prior permission from the Author. All text, photographs, and artwork are the property of the Author unless otherwise noted or credited.

The information in this work is true and complete to the best of our knowledge. However, all information is presented without any guarantee on the part of the Author or Publisher, who also disclaim any liability incurred in connection with the use of the information.

All trademarks, trade names, model names and numbers, and other product designations referred to herein are the property of their respective owners and are used solely for identification purposes. This work is a publication of CarTech, Inc., and has not been licensed, approved, sponsored, or endorsed by any other person or entity.

Edit by Scott Parkhurst
Layout by Sue Luehring

ISBN 978-1-61325-076-1
Item No. SA189P

Library of Congress Cataloging-in-Publication Data

Magnante, Steve.
  How to build altered wheelbase cars / by Steve Magnante.
    p. cm.
  ISBN 978-1-934709-26-9
  1. Automobiles, Home-built. 2. Automobiles—Chassis. 3. Automobiles—Wheels. I. Title.

  TL240.2.M34 2010
  629.228—dc22

                                    2009028510

Printed in USA
10 9 8 7 6 5 4 3 2 1

Front Cover:
With big-block power on tap, the author's Nova is able to launch hard and straight consistently and without drama. Careful design and execution of the modifications improved the quarter-mile performance without sacrificing street manners. (Mike Morgan)

Title Page:
With a vintage photo of Gene Snow's Rambunctious *injected Hemi Dart match racer for guidance, Dale used a plasma cutter and disc grinder to trim the fender for tire clearance. This same tactic was employed on the* Rampage, Kid Goat, *and* Corruptor's Pup *Dart match racers, so we're in good company.*

Back Cover Photos

Top:
Not to be confused with the one-and-only fiberglass-bodied 427 wedge Falcon of Dave Lyall (which was also red), the Carmel Ford Vindicator *is typical of many owner-built privateer Falcon match racers campaigned from coast to coast. Powered by a Hilborn-injected 427 wedge, the externally mounted Moon tank and flame-retardant silver driving suit suggest this one's running nitro.*

Middle:
The bottom edge of the quarter-panel patch is rolled under to match the existing profile. After final body work, the surgery scars will be invisible.

Bottom:
While the altered wheelbase drag cars of the 1960s were never intended to be street driven, modern design and craftsmanship make it possible! The sight of this pair heading onto the freeway in Southern California prove it can be done, and the joy of piloting such a car is truly immeasurable.

CONTENTS

Dedication 4

Acknowledgments 5

Introduction 5

Chapter 1: Funny Pages: History and Evolution of the Altered Wheelbase Door-Slammer 6
    Chrysler Funnies 14
    Ford Funnies 22
    GM Funnies 26

Chapter 2: *Wilshire Shaker* Nova Construction Overview 30
    Plan and Prepare for Surgery 38
    Move the Rear Wheels 41
    Replace the Front Subframe 44
    Prepare the Engine and Transmission 45
    Paint and Bodywork 47
    Install Front Clip and Straight Axle 49
    Apply Graphics and Install Engine 50
    Interior Details 52
    Fuel System and Loose Ends 54
    Test and Tune 56

Chapter 3: *Rampage* Dart Construction Overview 58
    Plan and Prepare for Surgery 59
    Move the Rear Wheels 60
    Install Subframe Connectors 67
    Relocate Rear Leaf Springs 69
    Install Mini-Tubs 72
    Upgrade and Narrow Rear Axle 74
    Install Roll Bar 78
    Install Straight Front Axle 82
    Install Engine and Transmission 88
    Install Hood Scoop 94
    Build Fenderwall Headers 97
    Apply Body Graphics and Lettering 99

Chapter 4: *Funny Fairmont* Construction Overview 111
    Plan and Prepare for Surgery 114
    Move the Rear Wheels 117
    "Swiss Cheese" the Rear Bumper 128
    Install Straight Front Axle 129

Chapter 5: Match Bash: Other Voices 139

Source Guide 144

DEDICATION

To the memory of Jack Sharkey, owner, builder, and driver of the Esserman Dodge-sponsored *Rampage* Dart of Chicago Heights, Illinois. Though Jack passed away in 1995, his legacy is perpetuated by Bob Millhouse and Shannon Sharkey-Millhouse.

ACKNOWLEDGMENTS

I wish to acknowledge the following individuals for their inspiration, guidance, and contributions: Roger Huntington for writing hundreds of great magazine articles on Detroit performance engineering; Sox & Martin, Don Nicholson, and the Ramchargers for presenting match racing as a truly professional enterprise; Roland Osborn, Cliff Gromer, and the late Steve Collison for giving me my "big breaks"; Ro McGonegal and David Freiburger, two pros I worked under during my time at *Hot Rod* magazine, who totally understood the Match Bash concept and allowed me to write extensively about it; Rich "The Performance King" LeFebvre for sharing many of his wheelbase surgery tricks; Pete "Mr. Hemi" Haldiman, Jim Kramer, Mike Guffey, and Dick Towers for their pioneering research on the subject of Chrysler altered wheelbase cars; and Dale Snoke, Dale "Can Do" Kutsch, and Phil Mandella for their expert welding and fabrication skills.

Any work of this nature would be incomplete without period photography to tell the story of the original cars and the brave men who drove them. Many thanks to Mike Ditty, Greg Fury, Doug Hayes, Chris Hood, Martyn L. Schorr, Bob Millhouse, and Shannon-Sharkey Millhouse for granting permission to reprint their original photographs.

—Steve Magnante, 2010

INTRODUCTION

You always remember the first one you see. With its mile-high stance, juggled body proportions, and vivid graphics, altered wheelbase funny cars are a shocking sight to behold. When they first appeared on the scene late in the 1964 drag race season, track owners and spectators alike quickly dubbed these wild creations "funny cars," thanks to their distorted appearance. But, there was nothing funny about their quarter-mile performance. The extra traction afforded by wheelbase relocation surgery put an end to wasteful tire spin, and quarter-mile elapsed times dropped by nearly 1 full second—with no other changes to the car or engine.

Add alcohol injection, nitromethane, and supercharging and these missiles could become quite thrilling—and dangerous. As with the early pioneers of land speed racing, supersonic aviation, and space flight, many racers paid with their lives in the quest for ultimate performance from a door-slammer race car. Regardless of the outcome, the awesome sight of two altered wheelbase funnies cutting a jumpy, smoking path down the drag strip will never be forgotten, nor will those who drove them.

This book is intended to spread the altered wheelbase gospel with a history review and by showing how three exciting Match Bash tribute cars—the *Wilshire Shaker* Nova, *Rampage* Dart, and *Funny Fairmont*—were constructed today using basic tools and skills. There truly is something for fans of every make. Even if your particular Match Bash project is based on a vehicle different from those outlined in this book, each section is packed with useful ideas, techniques, and tips you can adapt to your needs.

CHAPTER 1

FUNNY PAGES:
History and Evolution of the Altered Wheelbase Door-Slammer

The altered wheelbase phenomenon was in bloom for a brief window of time, late 1964 through early 1966—perhaps 30 months at most. But its roots can be traced back a full decade to the Detroit horsepower race of the 1950s. Starting with the 1949 introduction of the modern overhead-valve Cadillac 331 and Oldsmobile 303 V-8, successive years saw the arrival of a new crop of potent overhead-valve (OHV) V-8 designs in rapid succession, as competing automakers replaced pre–World War II flathead engines. Cars were getting larger and heavier, and extra motive power was needed. More significantly, the postwar buying public was nurturing an appetite for strong acceleration and sought excitement on the open road.

1951 saw the arrival of the Chrysler 331 Hemi. Then came the Studebaker 233, DeSoto 276 Hemi, and Lincoln 317 in 1952; the Dodge 241 Hemi and Buick 322 in 1953; the Ford 239 and Mercury 256 in 1954; the Plymouth 259, Chevy 265, Pontiac 287, and Packard 352 in 1955; and the AMC 327 in 1957. This first generation of V-8s planted the seeds for a vibrant horsepower race and each would undergo rapid evolution via increased displacement and breathing improvements as the magic 300-hp mark was sought and surpassed by nearly every manufacturer.

Les Ritchey's Mustang versus Al VanDerWoude's Plymouth at Irwindale Speedway, in Irwindale, California.

Some of these early V-8s quickly reached their limit and were revamped or replaced by better designs within a few years of their initial introduction. Others, the Chevy small-block and Pontiac in particular, were nearly ideal from the start and would remain in production for several decades with relatively minor changes, aside from increased displacement and the usual breathing upgrades.

As impressive as the first round of Detroit V-8s was, 1958 marked a turning point with the arrival of the so-called big-block engine concept. As the name implies, these big-blocks joined smaller V-8 engine types in many manufacturers' lineup and were called upon when the utmost in horsepower and torque was desired. Several carmakers introduced big-block engines, but the most significant to drag racing were the Chevy 348 W-series, Mopar 350/361 B-series, and Ford 332/352 FE-series. Each would grow from strength to strength and play an important role in the evolution of the muscle car in a few short years.

As the factory horsepower race escalated, racers and fans gravitated to the hot showroom stockers from Detroit. Though the early days of

NHRA, AHRA, and NASCAR drag racing were focused on a nearly infinite variety of owner-built hot rods, the new Detroit powerhouses of the 1950s spurred rising interest in stock-bodied drag racing. By 1957 most fans were just as excited to see a Pontiac Bonneville Tri-Power take on a Dodge D-500 as they were to watch a pair of blown dragsters square off. Each race stoked the flames of brand loyalty and strong life-long ties were formed.

Seeking to serve this growing segment of the sport, the NHRA created the first Stock class in 1955 as a playground for the new crop of Detroit machinery. At first, factory involvement was limited and the more sophisticated racers were sponsored, instead, on the dealership level. But as interest and participation grew, Ford, GM, and Chrysler became involved and offered special over-the-counter goodies to better their chance of victory. Typically these parts were from the export and police parts bins, or California-sourced aftermarket goodies that were blessed with a factory part number so they'd be considered legal in the eyes of the sanctioning body.

As the battle heated up, Detroit recognized the need to take things to the next level since corporate reputations were at stake. In addition, NHRA, AHRA, and NASCAR sought to control the previous free-for-all environment with stricter regulation of re-stamped aftermarket parts masquerading as factory-approved equipment. The days of swapping an Isky cam into a Chevy 348 and ruling the class were drawing to a close. New emphasis was placed on factory sourcing for legal stock class drag racing.

To establish a controlled environment, the sanctioning bodies formed competition categories with clearly defined sub-classes. The NHRA provided the first working model in 1959 with the introduction of its Stock Eliminator category. Advertised power ratings were divided by vehicle shipping weight data to determine where each Detroit stocker would compete. By establishing several sub-classes ranging from H/Stock all the way up to A/Stock, it was hoped that a level playing field would result.

Naturally, the outcome was that certain vehicle packages held an intrinsic advantage and would dominate—until the sanctioning body stepped in to rectify things. This game of cat and mouse between racers and sanctioning bodies continues today and debates will forever rage as the concerned parties split hairs over what is legal, less legal, and more legal. At the top of the NHRA heap came a category called Super Stock. Intended to prevent the more serious stockers from wreaking havoc in the amateur ranks, Super Stock quickly attracted plenty of direct factory interest. The Detroit super powers would draw the most potent weapons from their respective arsenals with which to defeat the enemy. This was war.

It is generally agreed that Ford introduced the first factory-assembled Super Stock engine package in 1960 with the optional 352 High-Performance V-8 for full-size models. Its 360-hp rating was a full 60 points above the garden-variety Thunderbird 352 Special, thanks to a high-flow aluminum intake manifold mounting a 540-cfm Holley four-barrel, 10.6:1 compression, big-valve heads, and beautiful streamlined cast-iron exhaust manifolds. Inside, the usual hydraulic camshaft was replaced by a solid stick with 306 degrees of duration and .480 inch of lift. Beefed connecting rods with wider beams and 13/32-inch rod bolts and a high-pressure oil pump relief spring added durability.

Only available with a column-shifted 3-speed manual transmission, the impressive 352 High-Performance was specifically designed and built to withstand the rigors of competition on the race track. By 1962 the Super Stock phenomenon was in full bloom and factory-engineered packages from Pontiac, Chevrolet, Dodge, and Plymouth had answered Ford's opening salvo. The common recipe employed by all factory Super Stock packages was the combination of the latest and greatest big-block engine technology with a stripped vehicle to maximize the power-to-weight ratio for explosive standing-start acceleration.

But good power-to-weight statistics are only part of the equation. It is key to recognize that *traction* is a vital ingredient in any effort to get a car moving as quickly as possible from rest. Big mile-per-hour numbers at the top end of the drag race are meaningless if the opponent beats you to the finish line. So, while Detroit dyno rooms were busy exploring the benefits of multiple carburetion, bigger ports and valves, hotter camshafts, and better intake and exhaust manifolding, chassis engineers were hard at work perfecting ways to take full advantage of the extra power.

Early developments included the substitution of the steel bodywork ahead of the firewall with aluminum and fiberglass in order to offset the extra mass of the big-block power plant, and as a means to juggle more static and dynamic mass away from the nose of the car onto the slicks for better bite. Trunk-mounted batteries became commonplace, and specially

CHAPTER 1

Pomona: If Only this Place Could Talk!

This unassuming ribbon of arrow-straight asphalt witnessed virtually every innovation, development, and breakthrough in the world of drag racing. From the first flathead rail jobs to run on "pop" in the 1950s to the factory door-slammer battles of the 1960s to the 330-mph Top Fuelers of today, the NHRA Pomona drag strip at the Fairplex in Los Angeles, California, is truly sacred ground. This rare shot from the other end of the strip was taken in the summer of 2008. The photo is deceptive. The famous starting line and luxurious NHRA tower suites are more than 1/2 mile from the camera.

calibrated front and rear springs and shocks were designed to encourage rearward weight transfer when the light turned green.

By 1963, factory studies in maximizing straight-line acceleration resulted in exotic machinery such as the Pontiac 421 Super Duty "Swiss cheese" Catalina and 421 Tempest, Mopar Stage II and III Max-Wedge, Chevy Z-11 Impala, and Ford 427 lightweight Galaxie. Once again, to prevent these NASA-grade machines from making mincemeat out of civilian pilots in lesser cars at lower altitudes, most were relegated to special Factory Experimental categories where they competed, high in the clouds among themselves. Although the Stock and Super Stock categories were exciting to watch and were still accessible to the average Joe, FX was the tip of the spear for door-slammer drag racing.

R.I.P. *Super Stock* Magazine: November 1964 – May 1999

It's been more than a decade since the chute was pulled on the once-mighty *Super Stock & Drag Illustrated (SS&DI)* magazine. Launched in November 1964, *SS&DI* played a pivotal role in fanning the flames as Detroit super stockers evolved into altered wheelbase door-slammers, then into all-out flip-top funnies. As the years passed, *SS&DI* covered other forms of drag racing and street performance thus adapting to changing times. In the mid-1990s the name switched to *Drag Racing Monthly (DRM)* to better reflect its role in the world. In its final decade, the late, great Steve Collison stirred plenty of controversy from the editor's chair and art director Todd Westover added an exciting psychedelic flair to the page layout. I am honored to have contributed several nostalgia-tinged articles before *DRM* faded into the sunset with its May 1999 issue. Today, paper collectors go nuts over vintage issues of *SS&DI*, with most pre-1970 examples selling for more than $20.

1964 was the breakout year; things went positively *nuclear*. The Mopar 426 Max-Wedge had reached the end of its potential so Chrysler released the incredibly potent 426 Hemi with 600 hp. Ford didn't take this sitting down and dropped the big Galaxie's 550-hp 427 High Riser into the compact Ford Fairlane, and the fearsome Thunderbolt was born.

As for GM, fears of anti-trust legislation spurred a corporate retreat from highly publicized racing activities in March of 1963, and all factory racing support was canceled. That didn't stop Chevy or Pontiac from continued performance development in 1964. The 409 was still available in full-size cars with solid lifters, dual quads, and 425 hp, though the aluminum body panels and 427 Z-11 engine were dropped. And don't feel too bad for Pontiac, which lit the fuse on the muscle car era with the hugely successful intermediate-size GTO. More street than strip, the GTO was a smash hit that took readily to hop-up tricks and contributed fat bottom-line profits for a decade.

Despite GM's lack of direct involvement, 1965 was the pinnacle year for outrageous factory-engineered drag race packages. Ford answered Chrysler's Hemi threat with a hemi of its own, the awesome 427 single overhead cam (SOHC). Mounting a camshaft above each cylinder head eliminated lifter and pushrod mass for a higher RPM ceiling. Several SOHC Cammers were installed in Mustangs, Falcons, and Comets for A/FX competition and some of the best match racing in history resulted.

GM enthusiasts were not paralyzed by the lack of factory-issue SS and FX machinery for 1965 and many built their own for non-sanctioned match racing. Plenty of blown and injected 421 Super Duty engines found their way into GTOs and Tempests while the new Chevy 396 big-block—suitably breathed on—was a threat when installed in Novas and Chevelles. In fact, Chevy managed to sneak 201 396-powered Z16 Chevelles out the door in 1965 with no ill repercussions. With an understated 375 hp in stone stock trim, many were transformed into Hilborn-injected match racers capable of giving any Hemi—Mopar or Ford—a close run.

Okay, let's get back to that all-important issue of *traction*. The Hemi revolution of 1964 created a dire need

CHAPTER 1

for extra traction. Mopar Race Hemi pilots were often forced to run on 7- and 8-inch slicks by class rules, and getting a clean launch off the starting line was always a problem, especially with a four-speed-stick transmission. Ford Thunderbolt and privateer GM racers were doing no better, and powdered rosin became a needed tool in the quest for adhesion.

More weight was needed on the rear slicks, but how to get it? Adding ballast was seen as counter-productive since increased vehicle weight diverts power to turn the tires. The trick was to shuffle *existing* vehicle mass. The quickest solution would have been to move the engine rearward in the chassis about a foot or two. Gasser-class racers took full advantage of this but since the stocker rules required an unmodified firewall, the Hemi had to stay put. Though far more complicated, the factory engineers—led by Ramcharger team members Tom Hoover and Jim Thornton—decided to shift the wheels forward beneath the body. The 1964 rule books did not list any specific prohibition on such actions, so the guys got started.

Contracting the Alexander Brothers of Detroit (famous for building several custom show cars for Ford and Dodge) to handle the chopping, the Dodge 330 Race Hemi Sedans of the Ramchargers and Dave Strickler were fitted with special tubular-steel front suspension control arms, longer torsion bars, and a repositioned K-member to extend the front wheel centerline 4 inches from stock. The aluminum front fenders were simply trimmed for extra tire clearance. Rear axles were also shifted forward by 5 inches via careful cutting and filling of the steel quarter panels, floor, and understructure. The final wheelbase dimension was 118 inches. A stock 1964 Dodge 330 rode on a 119-inch wheelbase so even though the net reduction was only 1 inch, the forward thrust of both axles beneath the body delivered 50/50 front/rear static weight distribution, even with the 720-pound Race Hemi sitting on the front tires.

A pair of 1964 Plymouth Race Hemi Sedans was also reworked for Tommy Grove and Al Eckstrand. Since the stock Plymouth wheelbase was 116 inches (3 inches less than Dodge), a different recipe was employed by the A-Brothers. Like the Dodges, special tubular front control arms, longer torsion bars, and K-member shifting were employed to move the front axle centerline ahead 3 inches. Thanks to the Plymouth's shorter stock wheelbase, the extensive rear suspension surgery and body modifications necessary on the Dodges were not required, and the rear axle was moved forward only

It's A Schorr Thing

Few magazine editors were as devoted to covering the altered wheelbase craze as Marty Schorr. Shown here adjusting the carburetor linkage on an aluminum-nose 1963 Dodge Max-Wedge, Schorr made certain the various Magnum-Royal publications under his watch *(Hi-Performance CARS, Super Stock and FX, Speed and Supercar, Rodder and Super Stock)* stayed on top of the match racing scene. Based in New York, Schorr's magazines were often in a unique position to cover eastern cars and drag meets the big California magazines tended to overlook. Collectors, historians, builders, and restorers swarm over Schorr-era Magnum-Royal publications at swap meets. (Marty Schorr Photo)

1 inch via special leaf springs and mounts. The end result was a 119-inch wheelbase and an equally advantageous static weight distribution.

The mini fleet of altered wheelbase Dodges and Plymouths went largely uncontested in 1964, though numerous magazine articles shed plenty of light on this ground-breaking traction trick. Performance was greatly improved as the altered wheelbase cars enjoyed reduced 60-foot times and regular high-10-second performance on carburetors and gasoline.

For the 1965 A/FX drag season, Chrysler pulled all the stops and constructed a fleet of six altered wheelbase Dodges and five Plymouths specifically for NHRA A/FX competition. Word was out that Ford's new 427 Cammer was capable of out-grunting the 426 Race Hemi. Combine that news with Ford's decision to drop the Cammer in mid-size Mustangs and Comets, and Chrysler was justifiably concerned. Hoover and Thornton devised an update of the 1964 altered wheelbase package. Following the "if some is good then more is better" philosophy, these very special 1965s were built with the rear axle shoved forward a whole 15 inches and the front axle centerline relocated a greedy 10 inches.

The final wheelbase was 110 inches and a 45/55 front/rear static weight distribution resulted in virtually unlimited traction. To maintain a visual link with showroom-stock Dodges and Plymouths, care was taken to blend the repositioned rear wheel openings into the quarter panels, and special fiberglass front fenders were fabricated to accommodate the revised front wheel location. Regardless, these things looked wild and ready for all comers.

Unlike the 1964 program, the 1965 fleet was built in-house by Chrysler employees working in a former Amblewagon ambulance-conversion facility. Initially fitted with cross-rammed 426 Race Hemis, the Dodges were campaigned by Dick Landy (*Landy's Dodge*), Bud Faubel (*Honker*), Dave Strickler (*Dodge Boys*), Jim Thornton (*Ramchargers*), Roger Lindamood (*Color Me Gone*), and Bobby Harrop (*Flying Carpet*). The Plymouths were campaigned by Butch Leal (*California Flash*), Sox & Martin (*Paper Tiger*), Tom Grove (*Melrose Missile*), Lee Smith (*Haulin' Hemi II*), and Al Eckstrand (*Golden Commandos*). A seventh Dodge was converted from a standard-wheelbase A990 Hemi sedan to altered wheelbase specifications by Dick Branstner's shop for Bill Flynn. Raced as the *Yankee Peddler*, this is the lone sedan in the 1965 factory fleet. The rest of the A/FX cars were based on the hardtop body style.

Chrysler may have focused too much attention on what the NHRA Factory Experimental rules *didn't* prohibit rather than what they did. When NHRA technical director Farmer Dismuke saw the Chrysler FX loophole machines, a new paragraph was immediately added to the rule book. It read, "Effective January 1, 1965, axles may be relocated on FX cars a maximum of two percent of the total wheelbase, per original stock location. This applies to either

See More on Video

To see the *Rampage* Dart, *Wilshire Shaker* Nova, and *Funny Fairmont* come to life on your TV screen, check out the 90-minute *How To Build Your Own Altered Wheelbase Funny Car* DVD. Go to www.thefunnycarfarm.com for details.

CHAPTER 1

Match Bash in Miniature

Can't afford to build a full-size Match Bash car? Maybe you just don't have the time and space. Either way, you can ride along by building a 1/25-scale plastic model. Kit makers AMT and MPC produced many classic altered wheelbase door-slammer models over the past 45 years. Some are very rare and expensive while others are currently being re-released and are priced modestly. Another option is hunting the Internet for the latest altered wheelbase releases from the resin-casting cottage industry. Or, you can scratch-build your own. Here's a trio of altered wheelbase machines I'm working on. The *Brutus* GTO is based on a vintage AMT kit, the Wood Brothers' *Palomino* Chevelle is based on a recent all-new tooling of the 1967 SS396, also by AMT. The (ficticious) Robie-Ford-Hilborn-injected SOHC match racer grew out of the recent AMT 1966 Fairlane kit. All have extensive wheelbase relocation surgery and borrow many parts from other kits. I get as much enjoyment building these miniature Match Bash cars as I do the big ones. You will too.

front or rear axle, or a combination of the two. Bodies must remain in their original production location. Wheel wells and fenders may be altered to permit installation and removal of wheels and tires but no portion of the tire may extend outside of the fender and/or body lines." Wally Parks' dominant sanctioning organization had seen enough and decided these highly specialized cars bent the already liberal FX rules too far.

With the stroke of a pen, the revised rule book barred the altered wheelbase fleet from participation at the NHRA Winternationals. To save the day, Chrysler hurriedly prepared four NHRA legal hardtops (two Dodge Coronets and two Plymouth Belvederes) with mild 2-percent wheelbase relocation for the Pomona race instead. Campaigned by Jim Thornton (*Ramchargers* Dodge), Roger Lindamood (*Color Me Gone* Dodge), Al Eckstrand (*Golden Commandos* Plymouth), and Tom Grove (*Melrose Missile* Plymouth), they ran the same 10.9s as the SOHC Fords and Mercurys but were not as quick off the line. In the end Tom Grove's Plymouth ran 10.96 at 126.05 in a semifinal round defeat by Bill Lawton in the Tasca Ford SOHC Mustang, which won with a 10.93 at 127.84 mph. At least the situation wasn't a total bust for the Chrysler boys.

But the altered wheelbase cat was out of the bag. The smaller, leaner, hungrier AHRA, UDRA, and NASCAR drag racing programs welcomed them, and the funny car circus was born. Chrysler brought many of the altered wheelbase machines the NHRA had shunned to the AHRA Winternationals for the January 29 to 31 bash at Beeline Dragway in Phoenix. In the cool desert air, the wild altered wheelbase Mopars delighted fans with wheelstands and mid-10-second passes.

By the midpoint of the 1965 race season, the traction advantage provided by the Chrysler altered wheelbase strategy was being applied to late-model race cars of virtually every make. Factory-assisted and independent drag racers alike learned there was plenty of money to be had barnstorming the nation's drag strips in no-holds-barred match race contests. Free from the stifling rules imposed during NHRA national events, racers made regular vehicle modifications and upgrades to stay competitive on the exciting new match race circuit.

Dual-quad carburetion gave way to Hilborn mechanical fuel injection, gasoline fell to alky spiked with nitro, and, finally, GMC superchargers entered the picture along with exotic super fuels like hydrazine. The motto was: "Run what ya brung, and make sure ya brung enough!" Most importantly, thousands of paying spectators were eager to watch the spectacle of brand-new, stock-bodied door-slammer funny cars running almost as fast as dragsters. Ford fans loved it, Chrysler fans loved it, and GM fans loved it. Make no mistake, these folks had never seen such a sight and winners could enjoy bragging rights until the next week's match race stirred the pot all over again.

And there were those wheelies! Fans just couldn't get enough of watching GTOs, Chevelles, Falcons, Mustangs, Novas, Darts, Belvederes, Coronets, and other popular "funnied" cars blast off the line, all twisted out of shape with the front tires 2 feet off the strip. Throw in some nitromethane and a blower and by the end of 1965, these wicked contraptions were running in the 8-second zone at speeds over 160 mph.

While the altered wheelbase treatment was a unique new development, many match race builders also borrowed a page from the gasser book by installing straight-beam front axles in place of the factory-issue independent A-arm layout. These straight axles didn't always weigh less than the factory stuff, but the simplified leaf springs supporting them allowed drastic increases in ride height. And as we all remember from high school physics, when you raise the center of gravity, more mass shifts rearward on acceleration, and the slicks bite in even harder.

Another benefit of the straight axle is that the front tires are immune to the radical changes in caster, camber, and toe exhibited by a stock independent front suspension when the chassis is exposed to massive horsepower. This means safer handling when the car does a wheelie as well as at the top end of the track.

The detail that's given many straight-axle cars a bum rap is the under-car airflow they encourage *when* guys take ride height to the extreme. Above 140 mph, airflow can separate the car from the racing surface and transform it into an impromptu glider unless careful aerodynamic tuning is employed. But for a typical sub-130-mph door-slammer the straight axle is a great choice. Any self-respecting funny car (the torsion-bar-equipped Chrysler 1965 fleet excluded) just isn't complete without the wild, nose-high stance it affords.

Ironically, the enhanced performance made possible by the altered wheelbase formula was also the core of its demise. Ever-increasing power levels meant increased trap speeds— as high as 160 mph. At these speeds, vehicle stability was no laughing matter and racers quickly sought a way to keep going faster without increasing the level of danger.

The solution came in 1966 when Lincoln-Mercury and Logghe Stamping unveiled a fleet of four Comet Cyclone tube-frame funny cars with flip-top fiberglass body shells. The cars delivered to Don Nicholson, Ed Schartman, and Ron Leslie were powered by Hilborn-injected Cammers while the Cammer in Jack Chrisman's topless roadster was fitted with a 6-71 supercharger. All weighed less than 1,700 pounds and the reign of the steel-shell altered wheelbase door-slammer was brought to a close virtually overnight.

Sure, plenty of teams soldiered on with door cars but by the end of 1967 you either ran a lightweight flip-top funny car, lost to one, or stayed out of their way by dropping to a lower class. As the flip-top formula took over, safety improved and many altered wheelbase former champions passed down the ranks as obsolete race cars and into obscurity. It was a sad close to such an exciting chapter in drag racing history.

But as they say, everything old is new again. Today any altered wheelbase machine is a surefire attention getter on the street or strip. Did I say street? Yes, I did! There's been a fast growing movement in the hot rodding world that's come to be called Match Bash. These cars are modern-day tributes to those early altered wheelbase door-slammer funny cars. But instead of 800 hp, they get by with 500. Instead of running breakneck speeds and flirting with aerodynamic disaster, high 10s at 130 mph do the trick and keep race track tech inspectors happy.

Most importantly, they're built with just enough taming so they can be driven on the street without breaking down, overheating, or leaving you stranded. Slowly but surely, Match Bash cars are taking shape all over the country and spreading enthusiasm for a time when funny cars had crazy altered wheelbases, opening doors, and steel body shells.

Before we begin the how-to chapters, let's have a look at some classic vintage machinery from the past.

CHAPTER 1

Chrysler Funnies

Butch Leal's California Flash Belvedere is another of the original 1965 factory A/FX machines. Note the profile of the large Dana 60 rear axle under this four-speed car. The automatic-equipped A/FX cars were fitted with Chrysler's less durable, yet lighter 8¾ rear axle. The lack of protruding injector stacks should not lead to the conclusion Butch was still running carburetors when this shot was taken. In 4-speed applications, many racers installed very short intake tubes on their Hilborn injection units to help move the horsepower and torque peaks farther up the RPM curve. These short stacks easily fit under the stock Race Hemi hood scoop without cutting. (Marty Schorr)

One of Chrysler's 1965 factory A/FX fleet cars, Dick Landy's Coronet started out with a magnesium cross ram mounting dual Holley 735-cfm carburetors and was the first un-blown stocker to break 140 mph in the quarter. Here he backs into the rosin after a burn-through during a match race engagement at Deer Park Drag Strip in Washington. Note the thin fiberglass door with its fixed aluminum window frame. Barely visible beneath Dick's helmet is a vertical push-button transmission shift unit taken from a 1964 Dodge. All automatic-equipped 1965 A-990 Hemi Super Stockers (and altered wheelbase A/FX cars) came from the factory with an awkward column-mounted shift lever. Landy's adaptation of the more user-friendly 1964 button shifter was a common modification. (Greg Fury)

As match racing set itself free from oppressive NHRA rules, racers quickly upgraded to Hilborn mechanical fuel injection as seen poking through Landy's lightweight fiberglass hood. With a straight shot to the intake ports and more precise fuel metering, injection added 50 hp over carburetors with no other changes. The greater benefit was its compatibility with alcohol and nitromethane fuels. With a 60/40 alky/nitro fuel load, Landy's Hemi was good for more than 700 hp and low 9's at nearly 150 mph. Notice the spindle-mount magnesium Torq-Thrust front wheels, a sure sign Landy has eliminated the weighty 10-inch front drum brakes fitted to the A/FX cars by Chrysler. A cross form parachute and 10-inch rear drum brakes provided the stopping power. Landy's Dodge was restored by noted collector Mike Guffey and still exists today. (Doug Hayes)

Home Wrecker: Chargin' *Chargers* on Tour

Match race success was all about maintaining exposure at as many tracks as possible. Then as now, professional drag racers lead highly stressed lives and are seldom home with the wife and kids. It can be a tough existence for everyone involved. As reported in the June 1964 edition of *Dodge News Magazine*, the factory-sponsored *Dodge Chargers* supercharged Max-Wedge drag duo was scheduled to run this mind-numbing, 22-date match-race tour from coast to coast during the summer and fall of 1964. Be careful what you wish for!

June 14	Niagara Dragstrip, Niagara Falls, New York
June 21	Charlestown Dragstrip, Charlestown, Rhode Island
June 28	Connecticut Dragway, New Haven, Connecticut
July 4	U.S. 30, York, Pennsylvania
July 5	Cecil County Dragstrip, Washington, D.C.
July 11	Aquasco Dragway, Aquasco, Maryland
July 12	Atco Dragway, Atco, New Jersey
July 19	Richmond Dragstrip, Richmond, Virginia
July 26	Newton County Dragway, Atlanta, Georgia
August 1	Golden Triangle Dragstrip, Tampa, Florida
August 2	Valkaria Dragway, Melbourne, Florida
August 8	Buckingham Drag Strip, Fort Meyers, Florida
August 9	Masters Field, Miami, Florida
August 15	Lake Land Dragway, Memphis, Tennessee
August 16	Little Rock Dragway, Little Rock, Arkansas
August 22	San Antonio Drag Raceway, San Antonio, Texas
August 23	Houston Drag Raceway, Houston, Texas
August 30	Continental Divide Raceway, Denver, Colorado
Sept 5-6	Rocky Mountain Dragway, Denver, Colorado
Sept 13	Albuquerque Dragway, Albuquerque, New Mexico
Sept 20	Fremont Drag Strip, Fremont, California
Sept 27	Henderson Dragstrip, Las Vegas, Nevada

CHAPTER 1

Dodge was toying with the idea of combating the 427 Ford Thunderbolts and Comets with 426 Max-Wedge-powered Darts in 1964. Jack Sharkey's Chicago-based Rampage (shown) and Billy Jacob's Kid Goat out of Enterprise, Alabama, were built to test the concept. The swapped Max-Wedge, iron-case 4-speed manual transmission and standard wheelbase resulted in a nose-heavy weight bias and tire spin, and restricted maximum performance to the mid 11s at 125 mph. Sharkey's and Jacobs' 426 Darts were described as private ventures by their builders in period magazine articles but it has since come to light that Dodge engineers offered extensive advice and free parts. Here Sharkey match races Don Nicholson's 427 High Riser-powered Comet wagon at Capital Raceway Park. Nicholson's mount is the only member of the eleven-car 1964 427 Comet fleet built on the 202 station wagon platform. With its 109-inch wheelbase (and obvious rear overhang) it enjoyed a significantly better weight bias than the 427 Comet coupes, which were built on a 114-inch wheelbase. Eddie Schartman took control of this wagon in the Spring of 1964. (Rampage Collection)

Not to be confused with the four Alexander Brothers-prepped Race Hemis of 1964, many standard A-864 1964 Race Hemi Super Stockers were given the altered wheelbase treatment in 1965 and 1966. Equipped with an Art Carr Torqueflite, here's the Goldfinger Dodge from Honolulu, Hawaii, in action at Lions Drag Strip in July 1965. Soon after, this beautiful car suffered a barrel roll during a match race. Driver Marc Danekas dusted himself off and continued racing the battered and bruised aluminum-nose Hemi 330 sedan the very same day. (Doug Hayes)

The front wheel location of Al Van DerWoude's 1964 aluminum-nose A-864 Hemi Belvedere sedan was unaltered. But by pushing the rear axle ahead 20 inches, weight bias results similar to Chrysler's 10/15 strategy were achieved. The only drawback is potential squirrelly high-speed handling resulting from the 96-inch wheelbase. The story of the Flying Dutchman's wheelbase surgery was covered in the pages of New Funny Cars, a 1967 publication that was part of the Popular Hot Rodding Gold Trophy series. It stands as one of the first altered wheelbase how-to articles to appear in print. (Doug Hayes)

Late in 1964 Sharkey replaced the Max-Wedge and four-speed with a carbureted Race Hemi and Torqueflite automatic. Further upgrades for 1965 included moving the rear axle forward 20 inches and installing a narrowed Dodge A100 van front axle assembly. The resulting 92-inch wheelbase allowed full traction and regular 10.68s at 132 mph. In this photo, the Dart is fresh from surgery and the distinctive Rampage graphics have yet to be reapplied. Sharkey eventually added Hilborn injection and ran 10-flat. (Rampage Collection)

FUNNY PAGES: HISTORY AND EVOLUTION OF THE ALTERED WHEELBASE DOOR-SLAMMER

Funny Cars: Not Always Funny

Between December 14, 1964, and May 19, 1965, 101 1965 Dodge A-990 Hemi Super Stocks were built. Although many were (and continue to be) campaigned on NHRA tracks with the standard 115-inch wheelbase, plenty were sliced and diced for extra traction. Sponsored by Big Daddy's Speed Shop of North Grafton, Massachusetts, Tom Parmenter was driver and Bob Blanchard was head mechanic of the Tom Terrific altered wheelbase Dodge Coronet. To simplify matters, the wheelbase surgery was confined to a 15-inch movement of the rear axle. The front suspension remains stock. Bob tells us the chassis work was performed inside an old tobacco barn in Hadley, Massachusetts. Another 101 Plymouth Belvedere A-990 Hemi Super Stocks joined their Dodge cousins in 1965. Unlike the Dodges, the Plymouths were all built before the start of the 1965 calendar year, between November 25 and December 30, 1964. (Bob Blanchard)

Young Chris Hood was only an infant when his father, Sammy Joe Hood, was tragically killed in November 1967 while driving the Hood, Heffner, and Potter *Hemi Cuda* match racer at the drag strip in Warner Robbins, Georgia. The car is shown here in 1966 prior to a radical rebuild that included stretching the wheelbase for improved top-end handling. Make no mistake, the nitro match race circuit was a dangerous place and its pioneers were very brave men. (Chris Hood Collection Photo)

Shown in action at Irwindale Speedway, Charlie Allen's 9-second nitro-injected Atlantic Dodge Flyer is a converted 1965 A-990 Hemi Super Stocker. Note the stretched rear wheel opening, a strategy that reduces post surgery bodywork by half since the trailing half of the wheel openings are not disturbed. The hastily trimmed front fenders are clear evidence the front wheels are moved forward several inches. The lack of vent windows suggests the presence of lightweight fiberglass replacement doors. The tall injector stacks were commonly used in Torqueflite automatic applications as they help boost torque output for harder launches. This car has been revived and exists today. (Doug Hayes)

CHAPTER 1

Frank Boggess' West Virginia Hemi Charger is a classic example of a Southern-style match racer. The elongated rear wheel opening isn't the result of shoddy workmanship. Rather, it's part of an ingenious, adjustable wheelbase layout featuring two sets of leaf-spring mounting points to allow a stock 115-inch wheelbase for legal S/SA racing or a 100-inch setting for unlimited match race duty. Similar adjustable-wheelbase strategies were employed on the heavily modified 1965 Plymouth A-990 Hemi sedans of Doc Burgess (Black Arrow), Merrimac Motors (Big Red) and Foster Mays (Wildcatter). (Marty Schorr)

No discussion of altered wheelbase machinery is complete without including the many experiments with mid-ship engine mounting conducted in 1965. More subtle to the eye than all-out altered wheelbase machines, several Darts and Barracudas were built across the country with their Hemis positioned behind the driver. Like most, the Hurst Hemi Under Glass was not initially built to do wheelies. Rather, George Hurst envisioned a traction-hungry match racer, capable of putting altered wheelbase machines on the trailer. But like the original Little Red Wagon, Hurst's Barracuda was too effective at transferring weight and proved to be hopelessly wheelie prone. Rather than fight it, the Barracuda (like the Little Red Wagon) was reconfigured and optimized as an exhibition wheel stander.

Bob Sullivan's Pandemonium started out as a radio delete, three-on-the-tree slant six 1965 Barracuda stripper—until he stuffed the blown-fuel 392 Hemi from his 7-second, 200-mph rail dragster between the fenders. According to the July 1965 issue of Drag Racing magazine it was completed in 27 days but the steel body, unmodified 106-inch wheelbase, and snoot-full-of-iron Hemi proved nose heavy, and lackluster 10.21s at 151.48 mph resulted. For 1966 Bob made some changes resulting in the car shown here. Instead of reducing the wheelbase like most match racers, he took an alternate route and added 12 inches to the front frame, thereby extending the wheelbase to 118 inches. The net effect is similar to moving the engine rearward in the chassis for improved traction, but the longer wheelbase adds stability at speed. A fiberglass 1966 front end—with repositioned wheel openings—replaced the stock 1965 sheetmetal. In this guise, Pandemonium was capable of running in the 9s at 160 mph. This car was recently resurrected and modernized for exhibition use. (Doug Hayes)

Fuel dragster veteran Tom McEwen joined the funny car circus in 1965 with the supercharged Hemi Cuda I. Based on a Formula S Barracuda (note the white racing stripe) a mid-ship 426 Hemi replaced the stock 273 4-barrel. Tom's rig was not wheelie prone like Hurst's creation and truly validated the mid-engine concept. The resulting 40/60 front/rear static-weight bias helped deliver its 1,000 horses to the track. McEwen wrecked it at Lions when it became airborne at over 150 mph but lived to build the nearly identical Hemi Cuda II that ran 8.90s at a staggering 180 mph late in 1965. (Doug Hayes)

Declassified Funny Papers

The Plymouth division of Chrysler Corporation chronicled the altered wheelbase modification process in Technical Report number 4208.7. Authored by H. J. McNichol, Jr., and released on January 12, 1965, the confidential document is titled "Race Car—AFX Dragster, A Series, B Body Plymouth." It consists of eight typed pages with sections covering Rear Modifications, Roll Bar, External Panels, Front End Modification, Control Arm Brackets, Torsion Bar Anchors, Front End Sheet Metal, and Welding. There are also 20 black-and-white photographs depicting various views of a 1965 Plymouth Belvedere body shell atop a rigid surface plate during modification. Copies are floating around on the Internet; it's a fascinating read. Can you imagine what Ford would have paid for a copy back in 1965? (Photos from Richard LeFebvre Collection)

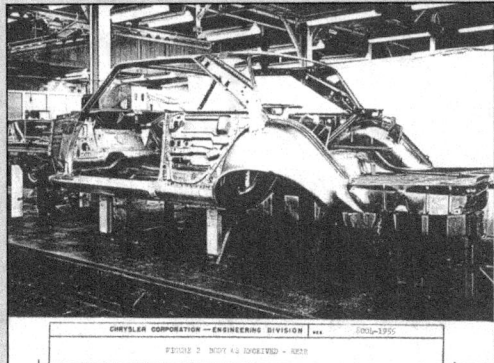
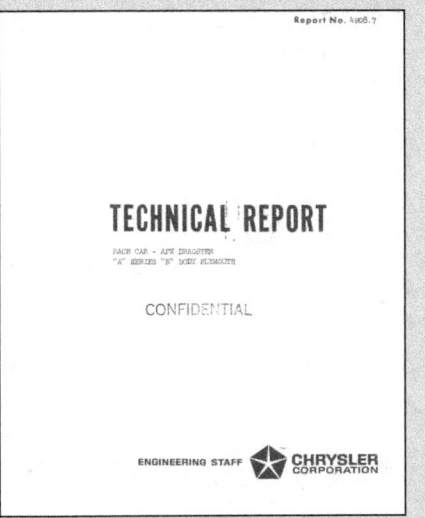

Pennsylvania racer Al Graeber bought the former Bobby Harrop Flying Carpet *1964 A-864 Dodge 330 Hemi Super Stock sedan when Harrop stepped up to a factory A/FX Dodge in 1965. Al transformed it into the* Tickle Me Pink *match racer with a radically altered wheelbase and Hilborn injection on nitro. By 1966 Mercury's flip-top Comets made the steel-bodied door-slammer obsolete, so Graeber stripped it and loaded the drive train into this 1,630-pound 1966 Charger match racer. Featuring a lightweight fiberglass body by Ron Pellegrini, Hilborn-injected Hemi, and push-button Torqueflite, it ran high 8s at over 165 mph. Graeber's Charger is typical of a transitional breed of funny cars built between late 1965 and early 1967. They combined the altered wheelbase treatment, steel tube frames, and non-hinged fiberglass body shells with functional doors. (Marty Schorr)*

CHAPTER 1

Plastic Fantastics

Of all the 1/25-scale plastic funny car model kits produced, two of the coolest are the AMT 1965 Dodge Coronet Hemi Charger (top) and JoHan 1966 Plymouth Fury. In a bizarre twist, neither kit is entirely faithful to reality. The JoHan kit's fault is the inclusion of a Sox & Martin build option as seen on the box. It is common knowledge the only full-size Plymouth C-bodies driven by Ronnie, Buddy, and Jake (King) were tow vehicles! In 1966 they were running an injected A-body Hemi Barracuda. The AMT Coronet presents a similar scenario. The Ramchargers' version depicted by the box art is a hardtop and has a standard wheelbase. They ran an altered wheelbase hardtop in 1965, right? Not so fast. Remember the four NHRA-legal 2-percent cars entered at the 1965 NHRA Pomona Winternationals? They were hardtops, so the box art isn't entirely wrong—even if the kit's body portrays the top-line Coronet 500. The Ram's Hemi hardtop was based on

To keep pace in the rapidly evolving world of funny cars, Graeber replaced the 1966 Charger door-slammer with this innovative mid-7-second, 200-mph creation in 1969. The front clip is removed from its multi-piece Fiberglass Ltd. body to reveal the Graeber-built, 120-inch tubular chassis and 480-cube, Hampton-supercharged fuel Hemi. In a feature story that ran in the September 1969 issue of Hi-Performance CARS magazine, Graeber says, "It's not a wheelie machine and I'm not a vaudeville entertainer. The tracks and spectators pay to see racing and that's what they're going to get from Tickle Me Pink." Speaking of wheelie machines, visible in the background is the stripped hulk of the former Bobby Harrop Flying Carpet 1964 Dodge Hemi. A priceless treasure today, it was nothing more than an obsolete parts donor by 1969. (Marty Schorr)

Fred F. Cain Chrysler-Plymouth sponsored this Massachusetts-based Barracuda in 1967. Packing an injected 426 Hemi backed by a Torqueflite automatic, the Hurri-Cain II is another example of the pre-flip-top transitional funny cars. Taking inspiration from the Ford-financed, Holman-Moody-built 1966 stretch-nose Mustang campaign, Cain's fish features an extensively lightened steel body shell perched atop a custom tubular frame and plenty of engine setback. Like the Holman-Moody Mustangs, the rear axle location is nearly stock but the front wheels are pushed all the way to the end of the fenders to redistribute more mass on the rear wheels for big traction. (Marty Schorr)

FUNNY PAGES: HISTORY AND EVOLUTION OF THE ALTERED WHEELBASE DOOR-SLAMMER

A Mopar through corporate marriage, the Ed Lenarth/Brian Chuchuas Holy Toledo Jeepster Commando is powered by a blown-fuel 392 Chrysler Hemi. By the time of its construction in 1967, 200-mph trap speeds were common and extended wheelbases were embraced as much for their calming effect on top-end handling as they were for placing more mass on the rear tires. This was Lenarth's second Jeep; in 1966 he ran the Secret Weapon CJ-5, also with a blown 392. The restored Holy Toledo shown here with the nose removed was photographed at Bakersfield in 2007.

The influence of the 1966 Mercury Comet flip-top match racers was felt far and wide and really signaled the death knell for traditional altered wheelbase door-slammers. One-time Mopar corporate relative, American Motors, launched a $1 million drag racing program in 1967 as a means to shed its dowdy economy image. The chief beneficiary was the flip-top Grant Rebel SST funny car built by Dave Jeffers and Bill Hayes with assistance from Grant Industries. Jeffers built it 6 inches longer than a stock fiberglass body by using an actual Rebel car borrowed from an AMC executive. The big surprise is the all-AMC mill. Based on a 343-cube V-8, a 3.75-inch stroker crank bumped displacement to 438 inches. Credible reports say it made 1,200 hp. Initially driven by Hayes, Hayden Proffitt later took the reins and ran an 8.11 at 180.85 mph. (Marty Schorr)

A look at the Rebel's highly sophisticated 121-inch Race Car Specialties tubular chassis stands in stark contrast to the primitive, cobbled altered wheelbase unibodies that were state of the art only a few years before. Koni coil-over shocks, a Corvair steering box, and Airheart rear disc brakes are among the high-tech features. Only the Dana 60 rear axle and magnesium Torq-Thrust wheels harken back to the days when altered wheelbase Mopars ruled the strip. (Marty Schorr)

HOW TO BUILD ALTERED WHEELBASE CARS

CHAPTER 1

Ford Funnies

Even though they were hand built at Holman-Moody's Charlotte facility, Ford's fleet of 10 1965 427 A/FX Mustangs fit the letter of the NHRA rule book and many appeared for duty at the Winternationals in Pomona. This is the second SOHC Mustang delivered to Gas Ronda. The first was destroyed in a crash after an axle shaft broke during testing in the weeks prior to the big Winternationals event. (Doug Hayes)

This pit shot shows mechanic Cliff Brien under Gas' Mustang performing maintenance between rounds. At the 1965 NHRA Winternationals this car defeated Al Eckstrand's 2-percent Hemi Plymouth hardtop, 11.06 to 11.21, but fell to fellow SOHC pilot Len Richter in the second round of Factory Stock Eliminator competition, 10.92 to 10.91 in a very close match. As per NHRA A/FX rules, which allowed a 2-percent wheelbase shift, the FX Mustangs feature a 105.8-inch wheelbase—versus the standard Mustang 108-inch wheelbase. Notice the enlarged rear wheel openings to accommodate the big Goodyear wrinkle-wall slicks. (Doug Hayes)

During the SOHC Mustang's sweep of the 1965 NHRA Pomona Winternationals, Len Richter drove the Bob Ford entry to victory over Jim Thornton in the Ramchargers "legal" 2-percent Hemi Coronet hardtop. Then he eliminated Gas Ronda's poppy red Cammer Mustang in round two. Richter went on to an unlikely victory over George DeLorean's Cammer Comet in round three. Though Richter twisted an axle shaft (the FX Mustang's weak spot) and coasted to a 23.90 ET, Delorean fouled and forfeited the race. Though set to face Bill Lawton's Tasca Ford Mustang for the final round, Richter couldn't make axle repairs in time so Lawton singled for the Factory Stock Eliminator trophy. Here Richter makes an exhibition pass at Irwindale during a 1966 West Coast match race tour. (Doug Hayes)

FUNNY PAGES: HISTORY AND EVOLUTION OF THE ALTERED WHEELBASE DOOR-SLAMMER

Mercury assigned Bill Stroppe's Long Beach, California, shop the task of installing 427 SOHC engines in four Comet Cyclones for A/FX duty in 1965. These cars were delivered to Don Nicholson, Arnie Beswick, George DeLorean, and Hayden Proffitt. Paul Rossi eventually took over the Beswick car (renamed Goldfender) so "the Farmer" could concentrate on his first love—Pontiac match racers. A pair of 427 wedge Comets were also prepared for Eddie Schartman and Ed Rachanski. Unlike the Holman-Moody SOHC Mustang strategy—which replaced the shock towers with horizontally mounted torsion-leaf front springs, the SOHC Comets retained coil-spring front suspension—but with the springs and towers repositioned outside of the engine bay. Proffitt's Cyclone was featured in the "Comet Wails" full page Lincoln-Mercury ad published in the August 1965 issue of Super Stock & Drag Illustrated and other enthusiast magazines. (Doug Hayes)

By the middle of 1966 the stuffy NHRA rule book was tossed out the window and Proffitt's SOHC Cyclone was optimized for match racing with an altered wheelbase and lightweight tubular front axle. Hilborn mechanical fuel injection replaced the dual Holleys and a heavy dose of nitro ensured mid-9s at nearly 150 mph—a far cry from the 11.2s at 126 mph turned during time trials at the 1965 NHRA Winternationals in legal A/FX trim. Here, Proffitt demonstrate the benefit of 45/55 weight distribution at Lions. (Doug Hayes)

Ultimate Barn Find: Hugh Baby's *Georgia Shaker III*

Most altered wheelbase match racers lived short, violent lives and were scrapped once obsolete or after one crash too many. Such was *not* the case for Hubert Platt's legendary *Georgia Shaker III* Falcon. Georgia funny car fanatic Tim Holland discovered Hugh's former mount in an old barn just as you see it here. Hugh was reunited with the 9.90-second, 140-mph stormer, and we all look forward to seeing it on the show circuit soon. The debate remains: restore or preserve? Either way it's a winner. (Fred Simmons Photo)

CHAPTER 1

Lions Drag Strip hosted the AHRA Stock Car World Championship Drags to a standing-room-only crowd of more than 20,000 paying spectators in August 1965. During runoffs for the FX/USI crown, Phil Bonner's SOHC Falcon pulled a giant wheelie and handed the win to Dick Brannan's Bronco Mustang. Based on a lightened steel 2+2 shell with fiberglass panels, the Mustang's rear wheels are moved ahead 10 inches, the fronts 4 inches. While the main fleet of 10 A/FX Mustangs were built to suit the NHRA rulebook, this was the first factory-backed altered wheelbase Mustang built specifically for freestyle match racing against the injected Hemi Mopars—or anything else that showed up in the other lane. Most of the construction was performed by Holman-Moody to Brannan's specifications. A write up in the November 1965 issue of Super Stock & Drag Illustrated magazine shows the car with a super-light fiberglass oil pan. This historic car ran 10-flat at 140 mph with carburetors (on gasoline) and served as the development mule for the 1966 stretch-nose Mustang fleet. (Doug Hayes)

After relinquishing his legal 1965 SOHC A/FX Mustang to Bill Ireland (who campaigned it with a wedge), Phil Bonner spent $20,000 of his own money building this brutal SOHC 1965 Falcon. Another Holman-Moody creation, the rear axle is moved 10 inches, the front wheels 3 inches, for a total wheelbase of 102.8 inches. Breathing through dual Holley carburetors, Bonner's Falcon was capable of defeating Mopar Hemi cars running Hilborn fuel injection and was feared wherever it ran. Bonner won 43 out of 44 match races, all the while power-shifting the Cammer at 8,000 rpm via a special aluminum-case Borg Warner 4-speed manual transmission. This is a Lions pit shot taken at the 1965 AHRA World Championship event. (Doug Hayes)

Hubert Platt campaigned no fewer than three 1964–1965 Falcon match racers—the latter two with altered wheelbase modifications. Since Platt ran with minimal factory assistance during this era, all were powered by carbureted or Hilborn-injected 427 wedges rather than more costly SOHC equipment. Regardless, Platt's quickest Falcon, the Little Georgia Shaker III, ran regular 9.90s at 140 mph and was a threat to more exotic Mopar and Ford Hemi machinery. This is the restored Iowa Shaker as it appeared at the NHRA Bakersfield Hot Rod Reunion in 1992. This car was campaigned by Tom Neeley after Platt's tenure. Platt's well preserved Little Georgia Shaker III was recently discovered in a Georgia barn by a lucky collector and will soon be revitalized.

FUNNY PAGES: HISTORY AND EVOLUTION OF THE ALTERED WHEELBASE DOOR-SLAMMER

Not to be confused with the one-and-only fiberglass-bodied 427 wedge Falcon of Dave Lyall (which was also red), the Carmel Ford Vindicator is typical of many owner-built privateer Falcon match racers campaigned from coast to coast. Powered by a Hilborn-injected 427 wedge, the externally mounted Moon tank and flame-retardant silver driving suit suggest this one's running nitro. (Marty Schorr)

This altered wheelbase 1966 Fairlane was originally conceived (and partially built) by Don Martin and Phil Bonner at Horsepower Sales in Atlanta, Georgia, as a 2,000-pound nitro match racer. The project stalled, and New Yorkers Bob Bowen and Ronnie Wacks stepped in and it was reborn as the Prestone Silencer, a gasoline-burning 2,400-pound AHRA S/US (Super Ultra Stock) entry. Boasting a Holman-Moody torsion leaf front suspension and special lightweight steel body shell, its 117-inch wheelbase is 1 inch longer than stock—though both axle centerlines are juggled forward over a foot for enhanced rearward weight bias. The 427 Cammer was initially run with dual Holleys (as seen here) but Hilborn injection was added late in the 1967 race season. A unique feature is European-style right-hand drive to place the weight of the driver closer to the right rear slick for extra chassis preloading. (Marty Schorr)

Though based on a highly modified steel shell, Bill Lawton's beautiful Holman-Moody stretch-nose Tasca Ford Mustang started the 1966 season running 9.70s at 140 mph on straight gasoline with a 4-speed stick. By the 1966 Indy Nationals, he'd switched to nitro and was running 8.60s at 165 mph with a C6 automatic transmission. The long 112-inch wheelbase resulted from shoving the rear axle forward 10 inches and extending the front frame rails 10 inches so the front wheels could be moved 16 inches. This dramatically improved starting-line bite and—just as importantly—high-speed stability at the finish line. Note the blocked-off headlamp recesses and streamlined gravel pan for improved aerodynamics. Similar stretch-nose Mustangs (with fiberglass body shells) were campaigned by Tom Grove, Phil Bonner, Gas Ronda, Darrell Droke, Hubert Platt, and Dick Loehr. (Doug Hayes)

Tom Grove's doorless Ford Charger Mustang was a state-of-the-art fueler in 1968. A far cry from the steel and fiberglass Mustang hybrids built by Holman-Moody just two years prior, it was proof positive that Mercury's pioneering 1966 flip-top strategy was the shape of things to come. Shown here immediately after construction, Grove's Hilborn-injected Cammer soon sprouted a 6-71 blower, and more appealing two-tone graphics adorned the one-piece flip-top body. (Marty Schorr)

CHAPTER 1

GM Funnies

Hiding in plain sight is the ex-Mickey Thompson 1962 Pontiac A/FX 421 Tempest. Originally built by Sir Mickey and Hayden Proffitt and raced by Lloyd Cox at the 1962 NHRA Winternationals in Pomona, don't confuse this car with the fleet of 13 factory-built 421 Tempests constructed in 1963. Though built with factory guidance, Thompson and Proffitt went freestyle and replaced the 1962's troublesome swing axle rear suspension with a narrowed full-size Pontiac axle and stuck an early 421 Super Duty beneath the steel hood. A nearly identical 1962 Tempest was built by Royal Pontiac in Michigan. Running on the class-mandated 7-inch cheater slicks, Cox defeated the Royal Tempest in this car with a 12.66, 115.68 mph run. By the time this photo was taken at Irwindale in 1966, a racer named Bob Porter owned the heavily modified car. The rear axle has clearly been moved forward about 10 inches, a Mopar Max-Wedge scoop has been added, and a straight front axle sits beneath the nose. Photographer Doug Hayes recalls that Porter used to tow the Tempest to the strip behind a sanitary 1932 Ford three-window coupe, which was originally built by Doyle Gammell, a legend in its own right among fans of historic street rods. (Doug Hayes)

Huston Platt's *Dixie Twister*: How the Mighty Fall

Brother of Ford hero Hubert Platt, Huston Platt's racing was done mostly in Chevrolet products starting with an aluminum-nose 1963 Z-11 427 Impala. By 1966 he was wheeling the altered wheelbase *Dixie Twister* Nova to regular 8.8-second quarter-mile passes at 161 mph. After a switch to a tube-framed Camaro, the Nova continued on the exhibition circuit as Max Smith's *Strange Stuff*. It was a severely outdated relic when Wayne Blanchard bought it in 1970 and parted it out. These three photos were taken by Wayne during the removal of the 466-inch Crower-injected L88 stroker in his Biloxi, Mississippi, garage. Nothing lasts forever! (Wayne Blanchard Photos)

FUNNY PAGES: HISTORY AND EVOLUTION OF THE ALTERED WHEELBASE DOOR-SLAMMER

Initially powered by a blown 421 Super Duty Pontiac, then fitted with a set of rare M/T cast-aluminum Pontiac Hemi heads, the Brutus GTO was built in 1965 by Lew Arrington and (pre-Jungle) Jim Lieberman. Piston problems and a broken valve—not to mention a scarcity of Super Duty parts after GM's 1963 withdrawal from racing—led to the eventual installation of a blown 392 Chrysler. The first version had a 10-inch rear axle shift with a stock front axle centerline. The resulting 105-inch wheelbase scared co-drivers Arrington and Lieberman at the finish line so the front axle was pushed ahead 8 inches and stability was regained. At 2,250 pounds, Brutus ran 8.8s at 164 mph. Lew Arrington sold Brutus to Don Williamson in 1968. In this photo, Don prepares the car for a day of action at Irwindale. (Mike Ditty)

Arrington replaced his steel Brutus GTO with this fiberglass Firebird for the 1967 match race season. Like all competitive funny cars of its day, Lew's new Firebird drew heavy inspiration from Lincoln-Mercury's revolutionary 1966 flip-top Comet program. Though the dwindling number of factory-backed Ford racers ran Cammers and a few die-hard Pontiac racers stuck with scarce Super Duty power, Arrington's Hemi-powered beast was part of the evolutionary change that put the plentiful and potent supercharged Chrysler at the top of the heap—and under the fiberglass body of most funny cars by 1968. Chevy racers were better off since the 427 big-block took well to supercharged fuel applications. But even they would make the switch to supercharged Chrysler Hemi power by 1971 in order to remain competitive. Detractors often called these cross-bred funny cars "wacky racers." (Bob Blanchard)

One of the greatest Nova match racers was Steve Bovan's blown fueler running out of Blair's Speed Shop. Bovan moved the rear wheels 8 inches and installed the straight front axle 5 inches forward to get more mass on the slicks. The nitro-guzzling 396 was set so far back into the firewall, a clearance notch was needed for magneto access. As the photo shows, time-wasting wheel stands and tire smoke were not a problem thanks to careful manipulation of mass. Backed by an Art Carr Torqueflite, Bovan punched the buttons at 7,400 rpm and ran 9.20s at 160 mph. Bovan sold the car to Ed Carter and Bob Little in 1967, who renamed it Chevy II Heavy and continued match racing it on the West Coast. Bovan moved on to a flip-top Camaro. (Doug Hayes)

Driver Richard Scott's flame-retardant silver suit was mandated on fuel cars like the Scott & Hunter Malfunction Chevy II sedan. Shown in action at Fontana Drag City in 1966, it's urged by a Hilborn-injected big-block backed by an Art Carr Torqueflite. The subtly stretched rear wheel opening suggests a 10-inch move and the centerline of the straight front axle appears to be 4 inches ahead of the stock location. The extreme ride height contributes to efficient traction as evidenced by the lack of tire smoke during this full-throttle launch. Chevy IIs and Novas were popular match racers thanks to their low initial cost and removable front clip (14 bolts), which simplified the funny car transformation process. (Doug Hayes)

CHAPTER 1

Another legend was Doug Thorley's Chevy 2 Much sedan. Photographed, here, at Lions in 1966, it packed a 700-horse, 481-cube Enderle-injected big-block running what Thorley described as "Tennessee Tonic" (nitro). Best of all, it was a four-speed-stick car! Based on a $600 used car, Doug invested $8,000 and three months to transform it into a 2,000-pound match racer with assistance from former (Jack) Chrisman's Comet crew member Dee Keaton. The altered wheelbase measured 98 inches (12 inches shorter than stock) and the entire floor and firewall were replaced with aluminum sheet. A feature in the February 1966 issue of Super Stock & Drag Illustrated says the Chevy 2 Much name was conjured by Ford pilot Hubert Platt's wife. Though initially plagued by violent wheelies, Doug added ballast and ran regular 10.07s at 144 mph. Doug built a replica that's currently on display at the NHRA Museum in Pomona. (Doug Hayes)

For every famous Chevy II match racer seen in the pages of a national magazine, there were dozens of lesser known cars running from coast to coast. Shot at Joe Vanni's 1966 Dover Dragway Super Stock Spectacular is the Westchester Automotive-sponsored New Yorker. Power came from a Crower-injected Chevy 427 running on gasoline. Note the rear axle centerline has not been altered. Instead, the builders chose to push the front wheels forward more than a foot. The result may not be graceful but it perfectly captures the true grit nature of these privateer match racers. Just a few names of the many notable privateer Chevy II match racers include Bruce Gowland's Howard Ellis Chevrolet injected 396 four-door from Canada, Mike Burkhart and Jim Kirby's High and Mighty, Harris & Robbins' Texas Bandit, Fritz Callier's CKC Chevy fastback, Grady Bryant's Sumpn' Else, Wes Jerde's supercharged Nova Too Late, the injected B/XS from Aladdin Casino, Elkins Bros.' Chevy Also, Randy Walls' Super Nova, Jack Robinson's Texas Twister, Al Oakes' Loehman Chevy II, Richard Schroeder's Bad Bossa Nova, Taylor Chevrolet's Hustlin' Hillbilly, Bill Stack's Arrow Speed Shop Nova, Jack Schaeffer's Honesdale Honker, and Jim Liberman's Mopar-powered Hemi Hercules—built prior to his legendary run of bowtie-powered Jungle Jim Novas. (Marty Schorr)

Brutus Gets Bashed

What happens when the intoxication of success (and nitro) has evaporated? In the case of the former Lew Arrington/Jungle Jim Lieberman Brutus GTO funny car, the road to obscurity started after its sale to northern California drag racer Don Williamson. Williamson had exhibition match race experience as a partner in the Hammons-Williamson-Hammons Hairy Canary 1966 blown-fuel Plymouth Valiant Hemi, so he was no stranger to their sometimes wicked ways. Sure enough, a young talent named Jimmy Trillo asked to make a pass in the car—and promptly stuffed it into the Irwindale guard rail. Williamson made repairs but later sold the car. Drag race enthusiast Mike Ditty snapped this shot that fateful day in 1968. Reports continue to surface that Brutus became a bracket racer in the 1970s and may still be in existence in some form. (Mike Ditty Photo)

HOW TO BUILD ALTERED WHEELBASE CARS

FUNNY PAGES: HISTORY AND EVOLUTION OF THE ALTERED WHEELBASE DOOR-SLAMMER

Funny Fifty-Five

Washington-state-resident Greg Fury worked at a small local speed shop in 1965 when Dick Landy came to town for an extended match race and wheelie show at Deer Park Dragstrip. During his two-week stay, Fury says, "Landy worked on his car in my shop and we talked a lot. He called the Chrysler factory many times and many parts were delivered to him in 6-gallon steel cans. He also returned used and broken parts to the factory engineers in these same cans." A racer from 1954 to 1986, Fury was strongly influenced by Landy's visit and built the *Lil' General* 1955 Chevy using the altered wheelbase strategy employed on *Landy's Dodge* as guidance. It's powered by a Chrysler 392 Hemi. Fury also campaigned a twin-Pontiac-powered rail dragster in 1961. (Greg Fury Photo)

Proving it didn't take a wild altered wheelbase machine to have a successful match race career, Bob Davis focused on the freak factor and the interest surrounding the new-for-1965 Chevy big-block with his near-two-ton Jolly Green Giant Impala exhibition car. Davis' Impala was factory built as a 396 4-speed but got a stroker crank for 480 cubes and was backed by an Art Carr Torqueflite (thanks to the popular C&O adapter kit). Initially Davis ran Hilborn fuel injection, but stepped up to a GMC 6-71 blower as a means to better motivate the Giant's 3,800-pound heft. Despite the stock 119-inch wheelbase, light fiberglass front end parts helped provide enough traction to put the blown Jolly Green Giant into the mid 10s. Davis poses with his super-size match racer at Fontana in 1966. (Doug Hayes)

Period magazine writers like Roger Huntington reported that Chevrolet toyed with the idea of building some Z-11-powered Chevelles for the 1964 match race season. But the corporate ban on performance activity squashed the program. Instead, independent racers took charge and built their own. Like Malcolm Durham, Dick Harrell, and Bures Hall, Bill Hahn installed a Z-11 in this Chevelle 300 two-door sedan. Yes, many Z-11 aluminum Impalas were sacrificed in the construction of these first-ever big-block Chevelles, but they played a vital role in keeping the Chevrolet flame alive against the many Ford Thunderbolts and Mopar Hemis they would face—and often defeat. As good as the 348/409-based Z-11 was, these pioneering Chevy match race teams switched their Chevelles to the more potent Mk IV 396 semi-hemi big-block when it became available in 1965. (Marty Schorr)

Malcolm Durham started strong in 1963 with one of the 57 exotic Z-11 aluminum Impalas and worked his way up to an altered wheelbase Chevelle—both of which were named *Strip Blazer*. For 1966 he defied Ralph Nader's published assault and constructed the wild *Strip Blazer IV* Corvair for the match race circuit. Motivated by a 427 Chevy, fed a 70-percent nitro load by Hilborn injection, Durham's Race Car Engineering shop retained the stock 108-inch wheelbase—but shoved the tube steel chassis forward 12 inches beneath the gutted steel body shell. Bucking the Torqueflite trend, Durham bolted a GM Turbo 400 behind the injected Rat. Later, an extra 12 inches were added to the front frame for improved high-speed stability. Other prominent Corvair match racers included Doug Thorley, Hayden Proffitt, Tom Sturm, and Pete Seaton. (Marty Schorr)

CHAPTER 2

WILSHIRE SHAKER *NOVA* CONSTRUCTION OVERVIEW

Some of the most popular altered wheelbase Chevys of the original match race era were based on the 1962–1966 Nova. With its compact dimensions, affordable purchase price, and lightweight construction, it was—and is—a natural for the Match Bash funny car transformation process. Drag racers packed their Chevy IIs and Novas with the exciting new Mk IV big-block Rat engine and hit the match race circuit.

These wild, quarter-mile contraptions, with great names like *Retribution II*, *Chevy 2 Much*, and *Sumpn' Else*, held their own against the dominant Mopar and Ford competition—most of which held the dual advantage of free-breathing Hemi engines and direct factory assistance. To be a Chevy racer at the time was to be an underdog. How times have changed!

Like every successful military campaign, municipal construction project, or moon launch, a Match Bash project should be thoroughly planned before you start cutting metal. A good tool to help formulate a consistent plan and help avoid missteps that dilute the impact of the finished car is to make a notebook diary.

The following is an excerpt from the handwritten build notebook I prepared to help guide work on the *Wilshire Shaker* Match Bash Nova. It's a machine that pays deep respect to the brave Chevy match-race heroes of yesterday.

Here's a before-and-after look at the Wilshire Shaker project. The wheelbase adjustment is both obvious and effective. The street manners have not been sacrificed, but the drag strip performance has been enhanced greatly. The visual impact speaks for itself.

WILSHIRE SHAKER NOVA CONSTRUCTION OVERVIEW

Today is November 9, 1997, and I've been at my new job at *Hot Rod* magazine for about two months so far and am pleased to say everything is going quite well. Sure, there are some adjustments and growing pains to cope with, but I'm sure it was the right move to say yes to *HRM* editor Ro McGonegal's job offer.

With the new-found financial stability that comes from this job I have decided to look into buying a cool car, perhaps with the idea of making it a project car for the magazine. My first inclination is to buy a cherry 5.7-liter Camaro IROC-Z. These cars are out there and good ones are still available. The same goes for a Mustang 5.0 LX sedan, my second choice in the initial search for a cool car. Then two things happened to alter my plan for a late-model project car.

First, I happened to see Dave Wallace's Hot Rod Nostalgia memorabilia catalog. In it was a book entitled *Match Race Madness* by veteran Texas drag racer Grady Bryant. I ordered the book and read the entire thing in a few days. Grady's accounts of his wild experiences as a funny car driver during the 1960s captivated me and within a few days I was fired up to build my own altered wheelbase match race car—but detuned so I can drive it on the street.

Then I asked around the Petersen offices to see if anyone had any cool old cars for sale. Dave Freiburger, then editor of *Car Craft*, had a neat 1964 Pontiac LeMans, but when *Hot Rod* magazine editorial assistant Mike Petralia told me of a 1963 Chevy Nova for cheap, I heard a bell go off in my head. I figured, why not do an altered wheelbase Nova for the street? The pre-1968 Nova really lends itself to funny-fication because of the 14 bolts that hold the front clip of the car to the firewall and cowl. Remove the bolts and the front end rolls away, ready to be replaced by a Bill Thomas Instant Funny Car kit, or a recreation thereof. Hmmm, tell me more, Mike.

Turns out, former *Hot Rod* staffer Will Handzell originally bought the car minus the drivetrain with the idea of making it into a magazine project car. He got a 1975 vintage 250 straight-six and air-cooled Powerglide and installed them just to get it running again. But Will lost interest, the car never ran, and it was sold to Petralia and his pal Marty, who intended to make it into a 9.90 Super Gas car. That was all back in 1995 and, before long, these guys lost interest and the car sat in Marty's mom's driveway with cats crawling all over it.

Yesterday, Saturday November 8, 1997, I drove to her house for a look-see. Their original asking price was $1,200, then $1,000, then $750. All of the price drops came without any attempt on my part to negotiate. These guys wanted the car out of that driveway in a hurry. A quick inspection confirmed the Nova's general excellent condition: It had original paint, no significant rust, some spare parts, and only minor dents. I said, "I'll take it" and gave them a $200 deposit and agreed to pay the balance of the $550 the following weekend when they delivered it to my house in El Monte. I'm Jungle Jim, I am!

On the following Monday morning, as I traveled to the SEMA convention in Las Vegas with editor Ro, I mentioned my plan to transform the Nova into a streetable altered wheelbase funny car and he said, "Do it for the magazine," meaning, do it for *Hot Rod*.

This will be a much simpler process than if I were attempting to restore the car. Less can be more and the objective is to construct a crude but clean tribute to all those famous 1960s match race cars without angering anybody with an unauthorized clone. I'll make it my own and want to go through the exact same construction experience as did Jungle Jim, Randy Walls, Doug Thorley, and others who built independent (non-factory assisted) Nova and Chevy II funny cars back in the golden age of drag racing.

So why a Chevy? It's no secret that Chrysler started the whole altered wheelbase thing with its various A/FX projects such as the Bill Flynn and Dick Landy straight-axle Dodges in 1964 and the fleet of eleven radically altered Dodges and Plymouths in 1965. But to build a Mopar would be to severely limit the popularity of such a project with the readership of *Hot Rod*. Let's face it, traditional *Hot Rod* readers are not necessarily Mopar fans, even one as intrinsically cool as an altered wheelbase car. To hang a lengthy series of build-up articles on a Chrysler product could be a risky way to fill the pages.

So to appeal to as broad an audience as possible, it must be a Chevy. Even a Pontiac (I briefly considered 'bashing Freiburger's 1964 LeMans) poses big problems. Yep, it's a GM product, but to be pure it'd need either a blown 392 like Lew Arrington's *Brutus* GTO or a super-scarce 421 Pontiac. Either way, it'd be way off the main stream.

But the Chevy II is valid because they truly were very popular match race cars. There were at least a dozen nationally recognized cars running in the 1965–1967 era with dozens more running under the radar of national magazine exposure from coast to coast and in Canada. My choice is made. Let's start a trend! Let's crack open the latest nostalgia trend—Match Bash cars! No billet! No braid! And a center of gravity just south of the Statue of Liberty!

Fortunately, the Chevy II has its own very well established aesthetic. By this, I mean there are enough published magazine photos of these cars from the altered wheelbase period that we can make accurate decisions today about what is correct and what is not correct in a tribute car. Just like Ford and Mopar FX cars, there is a generally agreed upon catalog of do's and don'ts that are particular to the Chevy II match race car. The Nova will provide me an excellent opportunity to spread the altered wheelbase gospel to *Hot Rod* magazine readers. This is gonna be fun! But before a single cut is made, let's make an outline of what the car should—and should not—be.

Engine

There is only one choice here, a big-block Chevy. Though a handful of small-block match race machines were on the scene in the 1960s—the Fiberglass Trends supercharged Corvair comes to mind— it took a Rat motor to be competitive with the Mopar and Ford Hemi machines in the other lane. Beyond that, Match Bash is no place for understatement and nothing says "GM's best and brightest" like a Rat motor.

Though the Chevy big-block is now commonplace, there was a time when it was the new kid on the block and much excitement surrounded its arrival on the scene during the 1963–1965 period. I'll capitalize on the "mystery," "Semi-Hemi," "Mk IV," and "porcupine" themes that were conjured by the press as it embraced the 409's replacement. I'll source a GM Performance Parts ZZ502/502 as the starting point. Got to paint the whole thing Chevy Orange, including the valve covers. It must look like the motor was just pulled from a 1965 Corvette, Z-16 Chevelle, or full-size passenger car—pretty much the only way to get one of these new motors if you weren't a GM employee in 1965.

Though a few match racers initially attempted to get by with carburetors on their Rat motors, the best visual impact is made with Hilborn injection with stacks poking up through the hood. Some cars did use Crower or Enderle manifolds with siamesed stacks, but I'll try to hold out for the evenly spaced stack configuration used on those first Hilborn intake manifolds. Evenly spaced tubes just look best. For street use, I'll ask BDS to convert the manifold to EFI.

Headers could be "zoomie"-style with individual pipes exiting beneath the engine or pointed outward. Maybe a bit too far for my streetable car and also flawed somewhat by the fact that zoomie pipes typically signaled an engine running nitromethane. Gasoline-fueled match racers used more conventional tubing headers with collectors. On my street car, this is pretty much required as I'll also need to plumb a muffled dual-exhaust system, though I'll do what I can to tuck it up close to the floorpan. Real funny cars didn't have mufflers! Sure, you could argue that those 1965 A-990 Mopar Race Hemis had that wacky crossflow muffler behind the rear bumper, but by the time these cars got their wheels shoved around by privateer racers for no-rules match racing, that muffler was long gone.

I'll run a stock water pump and alternator for street suitability. Billet aluminum parts are strictly forbidden. For those nit-pickers who may cry foul about an injected motor without the traditional cast-aluminum timing chain cover and cam-driven fuel pump, remember that those very early Hilborn injection setups also were available with belt-driven fuel pumps that mounted like a power steering pump at the front of the engine. There are plenty of magazine hits showing Mopar Race Hemis with the stock water pump, alternator, clutch fan, and pulleys but with a belt-driven Hilborn pump sharing the space.

Transmission

There's a 25-percent chance I'll run a 4-speed manual transmission. It would be sexy as heck but complicated to get the clutch linkage set up. There is a 25-percent chance I'll run a cable-operated Chrysler 727 Torqueflite with the buttons sticking out of a pod in the car. The C&O Torqueflite-to-Chevy kit is probably long gone. Does anybody else make one? Plus I'll have to find a 1965 cable-operated Torqueflite and swap the input shaft so I can use a modern 1968-up torque converter. Hmmm, kind of complicated. There is a 50-percent chance I'll just run an out-of-the-box B&M Turbo 400 with manual valve body and a lever-type shifter on the floor. The shifter itself could be vintage Pontiac or pretty much any mid-1960s console-type unit, but the shift handle must remain stock so it looks right. No modern aftermarket shifters are allowed! The Turbo 400 would be the easy way out.

Front Suspension

The stock Nova/Chevy II frame and suspension clip is definitely out! Way too narrow between the spring towers, too heavy, and very difficult to rework into altered wheelbase status. The obvious choice is to go with an original, or recreated, Bill Thomas Instant Funny Car tube frame clip with semi-elliptic leaf springs and a straight axle. This is a beautifully simple design and there are dozens of photo out-takes in the *Hot Rod* photo archives showing the intricate details if an original one cannot be located. I recall seeing one for sale at the Super Chevy show in Pomona in 1995 or so. Maybe there is one floating around someplace?

The front wheels can't be shoved forward too much due to the already-forward positioning of the stock Nova wheel openings in the fenders. A possible way out would be to stretch the front fenders like on the 1966 Ford Mustang AFX fleet. Remember, if the fenders get stretched and are longer than stock, the front frame clip must also be stretched to match. So if I unearth an original Bill Thomas kit, it'll need to be reworked to suit. This would negate the bolt-on convenience factor. Also, the stretch-nose look may, or may not, work on the somewhat stubby Nova. The Wood Brothers Palomino 1966 Chevelle got a sickening stretch nose that is unbelievably strange to look at. I like it, but it's a very bold statement. Think this over a bunch!

Back to the Bill Thomas kit, vintage articles in both *Hot Rod* and *Rod & Custom* say it moves the front wheel centerline forward 3 inches. How should the wheel openings be handled to make tire clearance? I'll take my cue from the March 1966 issue of *Hot Rod* in Jim McFarland's story, "A Novel Nova." In it the lower edges of the fenders are trimmed, resulting in a cool "busting out" appearance.

A grotesquely interesting alternate possibility is seen in the Westchester Automotive-sponsored New Yorker, a 1964 A/FX Chevy II that has the front axle pushed at least 1 full foot forward. To make room, the builders simply cut the bottoms of the front fenders completely off and eliminated the front bumper. The look is almost cartoonish. Think twice on this one because without a front bumper and sitting so high in the air, traffic police are far more likely to take notice and enforce vehicle code violations. Remember, this will be a street car! Still, the ride height must be increased several inches over stock to get the desired shocking visual effect.

Engine Setback

The Bill Thomas setup would allow for a great range of motor positioning flexibility. Try to get the injector stacks way back into the cowl vent area, but not so far that the windshield needs to be cut. Before he drove the *Brutus* GTO for Lew Arrington, Jungle Jim Liberman had an injected Hemi-powered Chevy Nova called *Hercules*. In the January 1966 issue of *Super Stock & Drag Illustrated* there is an excellent photo on page 23 showing the massive engine setback, as well as a pair of great launch pictures of the *Hercules*.

Such engine setback will necessitate firewall and floorpan cutting and filler fabrication. This is where a four-speed manual transmission starts to get more complicated than it is worth. Imagine the clutch linkage fabrication nightmares. Aluminum is cool for patching the holes and reconstructive work on the floor, cowl, and transmission tunnel. Just avoid quarter-turn fasteners and artsy-fartsy, embossed bowtie designs and heavy perimeter beads, as such details were not found on these cars. It was only after the arrival of the tubbed Pro Street movement in the late 1970s that chassis fabricators started inflicting these modern flourishes on their subjects. Steer clear—keep it crude but clean.

Then again, maybe there should not be any engine setback. There are numerous photos of cars with stock firewalls and stock engine location. Richard Schroeder's *Bad Bossa Nova* and Dickie Harrel's 1966 both looked wild with their injector stacks sticking through their hoods, but they both had stock firewalls! Think this over. With the altered wheelbase and 502-hp, this thing is going to have great weight transfer. But if the motor is set back 10 inches or so, it might cross the line and become an unpleasant, self-destructive wheelie machine. Consider this seriously! But if the plan to do engine setback wins out, check out the March 1966 issue of *Hot Rod*, the "Novel Nova" story has great detail photos of how it can be done. It looks fairly easy.

Rear Suspension

I'm definitely leaning toward leaf springs with Ford Thunderbolt-style lift bars, but remember, if these bars are welded to the axle tubes, they will be subjected to twisting forces as the body rolls from side to side on corners that could cause fatigue of the welds and tubes. Think this over. I'm also pretty sure the stock Nova mono-leaf springs (or reworked versions of the same) will not provide the required ride height increase, so I'll probably use a set of Chrysler Super/Stock leaf springs. Also, I like the idea of using Chrysler springs in this Chevy because it pays tribute to the fact that Mopar A-990 leaf springs were often transplanted into non-Mopar funny cars. You see it all the time in the old magazines.

The rear axle will be a Ford 9-inch. Must be the early style with the smooth face because this is the style used on the Ford factory drag cars, from the 406 to the Thunderbolt to the SOHC 1965 Mustang A/FX-ers. Yes, the later bulge-style housing does appear on the 1966 flip-top Mercury funny cars, but I'll go with the early smooth-face

Magnesium Five-Spokes Return!

Look at vintage photos of altered wheelbase match race machines and you'll see many running on skinny magnesium front wheels. Manufactured by American Racing Equipment, the original 15 x 4-inch Torq-Thrust five-spoke mag was once a popular wheel but has since become a scarce commodity. Most seekers today are forced to settle for close-but-no-cigar 15 x 4.5-inch aluminum Torq-Thrust-D front runners for their retro Match Bash cars, gassers, and traditional hot rods. But, thanks to Ray Franklin's Vintage Engineering, you can get brand-new magnesium 15 x 4-inch five-spoke wheels in the popular bolt patterns. They aren't cheap but sell for less than what most swappers ask for original wheels. The big difference is that Ray's five-spoke wheels are brand-new, not battle-worn relics with untold duty cycles and frequent corrosion issues. This Vintage Engineering 15 x 4-inch five-spoke is a dead ringer for the original and adds a period-correct finishing touch to any Match Bash car.

type for my Nova. I'll fill the housing with good 31-spline axles and a Traction Lock or Detroit Locker differential with street-oriented gears, probably 3.89s.

How much to move the rear axle? Typical Chevy II funny cars shown in the old magazines have a wide range of movement possibilities. Some show virtually no relocation, just a full radius job on the wheel opening to make room for the slicks. Others show what looks to be as much as 12 inches of relocation. The ultimate dictator of how far you can go is the amount of "real estate" between the front of the wheel opening and the door sill and jamb.

I'll follow the tasteful pattern set by Dick Harrell's 1966 Nova and go with 8 inches. It will be enough movement to be obvious that something has been done to the car without treading into the realm of the grotesque. I definitely want to avoid the circus-car look like Al Van Der Woude's poor 1964 *Flying Dutchman* Plymouth. Make no mistake, grotesque can be good; I just want this high-profile *Hot Rod* magazine project car to be classy and well proportioned rather than freakish and off-putting to the untrained eye.

Who's going to move the rear axle? Not me; I can't weld. But I can probably get it done locally for $1,000 or so. It must be period correct. Don't allow the chassis fabricator to talk me into aluminum tub work, a four-link suspension system, coil-over shocks, or any other nonsense that would dissipate the illusion that this car was built in 1966.

The wheel openings will need to be dealt with too. There are two ways to go. The first would be to follow the factory Chrysler plan and move the rear wheel openings intact. This calls for filling in the space left behind, which in itself poses the difficulty of restoring a smooth, graceful line at the bottoms of the quarter panels.

The alternative would be to simply stretch the wheel opening so that the leading edge and the trailing edge remain unmolested. This eliminates the issue of how to retain an attractive profile, because the stock lines are not altered. This stretched wheel opening treatment delivers a very shocking "butch" appearance and makes it clear to even casual observers that the wheels have been repositioned. Going too far can be ugly in a beautiful way. A great example of this is how Don Nicholson's 1965 SOHC Comet got a similar treatment when it was updated for 1966. I like the look; this could be the way to go.

Brakes

Though the first altered wheelbase 1964 and 1965 Mopar Hemi drag cars used 10-inch front and rear manual drum brakes, the front brakes were quickly discarded and replaced with parachutes and spindle-mount mag wheels. But for my street-going Nova, I've got to bend the rules a bit. Up front I will merge some discrete aftermarket disc brakes with the straight axle to give the car safe stopping capabilities.

At the rear axle, I'll stay true and go with drum brakes. There are aftermarket rear disc brake kits available for virtually all axle types, but to my eye, they are too modern and spoil the retro vibes. Plus, you've got to remember that the area between the spokes of most mag wheels will reveal your choice of brakes. Make it the right choice. And beyond that, a popular treatment in the 1960s was to paint the brake drums a bright color. With disc brakes this opportunity is lost and bright painted calipers don't count. Blinged-out brake calipers are a decidedly modern Honda/import tuner detail that has no place on a retro Match Bash car.

I will convert the Nova from its single-pot master cylinder to a dual-circuit master cylinder from a 1967 Nova. It bolts right onto the firewall and accepts the stock brake pedal. The hand brake can most likely be retained, though merging the stock Chevy cables to the Ford brake backing plates may require some ingenuity.

Wheels

About the only thing I know for sure is that the wheels will have the Ford/Mopar 5-on-4½ bolt circle, so as to fit the anticipated Ford 9-inch rear axle. The rims will be 15 inches in diameter. A bunch of wheel designs are eligible here, but as with the rest of the car, any wheel designed after 1967 is strictly forbidden. The list of non-acceptable wheels is much longer than the list of acceptable wheels. There is no faster way to ruin the mood of a retro car than to use modern-era wheels. The wheels alone can make, or break, the illusion of being transported back to Cecil County Drag-O-Way or Beeline, circa 1966.

Possible candidates for the Nova include American Racing aluminum Torq-Thrust-D, aluminum flat-spoke Torq-Thrust, magnesium flat-spoke Torq-Thrust, 12-spoke spindle mount (front only), Cragar S/S, magnesium Halibrand 5-hole (large window), and stock stamped steel wheels. Generally the front rims should be no wider than 5 inches, with 4 inches being preferred. The rear rims must not be wider than 8 inches, as wider rims are rarely seen in 1960s photos of full-body altered wheelbase match racers.

I must consider the present-day availability of whatever wheels are chosen. I am leaning toward either the American Racing aluminum Torq-Thrust-Ds (15 x 4.5 and 15 x 7) or Cragar S/Ss (15 x 4.5 and 15 x 7) because both are still available new and are reasonably priced. True vintage American Racing mag wheels can be very expensive these days.

Tires

No radial tires! Just like wheels, the wrong tire selection can have a dulling effect on the success of the entire project. Too many retro Super Stock builders and muscle car restorers blow it by taking the knee-jerk radial tire route. I've driven plenty of cars equipped with bias-ply tires—as did millions upon millions of Americans prior to the widespread arrival of radial tires in the 1970s—and have concluded that bias-ply skins are perfectly acceptable for sane street use and high-speed, straight-line (drag racing) use.

The only drawback is that most bias-ply tires are not rated for sustained high-speed driving, so wide-open highway driving at speeds in excess of 100 mph is not advisable. Knowing that such antics fall well outside the Nova's intended use, I'll go with tall bias-ply black walls up front.

At the rear of the car, aside from the letter markings and name brands, modern wrinkle-wall slicks have about the same look as the first generation of wrinkle-walls that appeared in late 1965. Thus I could use 10-inch-wide M&H or M/T slicks on the back and get an acceptable look (though the white stenciled manufacturer logos must be removed for period-correct vibes).

But this is a street car, remember? Wrinkle-wall slicks have many drawbacks on the street. First, the soft rubber compound attracts sharp objects and invites punctures. Second, the thin sidewall construction that works to cushion the connection between the rim and the tread to help prevent tire spin also allows severe lateral sway in cornering situations. Finally, the treadless design is deadly on wet pavement, as water has no place to escape so the tire loses contact with the pavement and hydroplaning results.

A solution to two of these drawbacks would be to go with some of the new retro-styled M/T square-shoulder slicks. They have thick sidewall construction that minimizes deflection to eliminate side-sway, and the hard rubber compound resists damage and provides much longer tire life. The only drawback is the treadless design that'll make wet weather driving very hazardous. But then again, will I really be driving this car in the rain? Is this really such a big issue? Maybe I could get grooves cut into the tires by one of the local truck tire re-grooving shops.

Modern M&H, Hoosier, or M/T D.O.T.-approved soft-compound slicks are a last-resort option. These tires will not attract the attention of law enforcement officers like pure slicks will, but even though they are belted-type tires, I just can't accept their looks, especially the ones with rounded shoulders and overdone tread patterns that would look at home on a mud-bog truck. True slicks of some type will likely get the nod.

Body and Frame

The plan is to retain the basic steel shell (with rear wheel relocation) and use fiberglass fenders, hood, front bumper, and maybe trunk lid. The fiberglass hood must be the stock flat type with no scoops, blisters, or cowl induction replicas. Though Ford Thunderbolt-style hood blisters appeared occasionally on non-Ford match race cars, I'll follow the predominant pattern and stick with a flat hood with a neat hole cut for injector tube clearance once I know where they will be.

The doors will probably remain steel because I'm not really going for maximum weight reduction on this street car. Fiberglass doors are a super bummer in everyday use. They rattle, suffer from wind noise, aren't water tight, and rarely fit well.

The rear bumper should remain steel, as most door-slammer funny car racers wanted weight at the rear of the car to help plant the slicks. So weight reduction isn't really as critical behind the rear axle centerline as it is ahead of it. Still, the chromed-steel rear bumper allows the use of a stunning visual trick. I'll use a hole saw to put a series of "Swiss cheese" holes in the bumper like those seen on the Hodgson and Mills Canadian Nova A/XS. It's super cool.

Because this is to be a street car that might even go on the Hot Rod Power Tour cross-country drive, I'll employ a level of fit, finish, and weather resistance not often seen on the old match racers. The windshield and backlight will remain glass to ward off scratches, though it sure would be great to be able to recreate the wild "Swiss cheese" air vent holes used on the plexiglass rear window and rear side windows of so many funny cars. The *Brutus* GTO had an awesome display of this. But again, all those holes will admit copious amounts of water and road grime, and force the use of delicate plastic windows. I'll think this over...

Though the Chevy II is a unit-construction car, the floorpan is among the thinnest, most lightweight I've ever seen. The rocker sills are not even boxed. By comparison, a Dodge Dart is an absolute tank. As such, it might benefit from a welded tubular steel helper frame of the type depicted in the 1966 *Drag Strip* magazine feature on Steve Bovan's *Blair's Speed Shop* supercharged 1964 Chevy II match racer. This arrangement consists of a series of longitudinal and lateral tubes that form a truss that coexists with the stock Nova floor metal and integrated subframe sections. It is a little complex. Would it really be needed on my un-blown street car? Bovan's fuel Nova probably made nearly 1,000 hp, about twice what I'm planning. A less drastic option is to install a basic weld-in frame connector kit of the type that welds to the front and rear subframe segments.

Paint & Graphics

This is a puzzler. On one hand I'd love to revisit the look of a classic Chevy match racer...how about the orange-and-white two-tone effect used on the *Seaton's Shaker* Chevelle and Corvair funny cars? Or the emerald green metalflake used on Richard Schroeder's *Bad Bossa Nova*? Interesting but definitely out is the lurid bright yellow of Randy Walls' supercharged Super Nova. Sorry, but it has been stereotyped by the mind-numbing parade of yellow hot rods. It's just too obvious at this point in time.

The term "graphics" has all-too-often come to mean tasteless stripes and tacky pastel wisps slathered about the body with little regard for the lines of the car they are applied to. Not so with my Nova. I'll let history be my guide and have period-correct lettering applied—by hand, with a brush—to give the Nova its own distinct personality. There won't be any attempt to duplicate the actual paint and lettering of any particular race car. Rather, I'd riff on the details but make them my own.

On the other hand, there is something to be said for a more basic presentation. Two-tone custom paints and lettering can be a win-or-lose proposition and it might be easy to go too far. And, once the paint is applied, you can't really take it off. I'm also thinking that the altered wheelbase and injector stacks might work just as effectively if the car is painted a single color. Maybe white, red, or some other stock Chevy Nova paint hue. But would this be too bland? I'm not sure yet.

Interior

Richard Schroeder's *Bad Bossa Nova* sets the tone. On page 19 of the October 1966 issue of *Drag Strip*, the interior of this gorgeous green 1966 Chevy II is revealed. It has a single Mopar A-990 seat with the stock aluminum mounting brackets! It's champagne colored, signifying it came from a 1965 Mopar Hemi car—a red seat would have come from a 1964 Hemi Mopar. So in tribute, I'll get a pair of A-100 Dodge van bucket seats and see Jim Kramer for some reproduction A-990 brackets. Hey, if an ex-Mopar Super Stock seat was good enough for Schroeder's Nova, it'll be right at home in this *Hot Rod* magazine project car. I dig the opportunity to demonstrate that Chrysler-sourced parts wound up in a lot of non-Chrysler match racers back in the day.

Schroeder's Nova also sets the tone for interior trim…there is none! His car was gutted. The dash is stock metal but nothing is left other than a bunch of crude holes. The same goes for the doors; the interior panels are gone, leaving the skeletal inner door structure for all to see. The headliner is also gone. Unity is restored by a liberal application of GM spatter-coat trunk paint on virtually every interior surface. I'll strip my Nova too, but will retain the stock instrument cluster. It is compact and simple enough, plus it'll be helpful to have a functioning fuel gauge and speedometer. Remember, this will be a street car! One must-have item that I will find is a bona-fide radio delete plate.

Roll Cage

To abide by safety rules and pass drag strip tech inspection, an 8-point roll bar will be installed to restore and enhance rigidity. After all, this thing will probably run into the low 11s with its anticipated 500 hp. Do not allow the roll bar to become too modern. Don't get talked into a full cage or down bars that follow the A-pillar. A simple 8-point roll bar is good enough up to the 11.00-second ET barrier, where the NHRA wants to see a full cage. A basic Simpson or Deist 5-point safety harness will be installed but it must have black webbing. There will be no import-tuner-style electric blue, red, or neon yellow safety harnesses allowed!

Fuel System

Most match race Novas I've studied have either a small Moon tank or a minimal-capacity motorboat fuel tank fastened to the trunk floor. I'd like to be true to this fact but must overrule it in favor of a stock 16-gallon Nova fuel tank for increased range and to support the street-driven premise. But will a fully topped gas tank become a wheelie-making ballast box? Hope not. All the same, I'll run a stock gas tank and keep the trunk compartment empty except for a Mopar Super Stock battery. A classic mistake would be to just go with a plastic fuel cell in the trunk. Can't do it; they simply didn't exist back in the 1960s and to my eye, they're kind of ugly.

Electromotive will most likely be providing the EFI system for the motor. This will likely include an in-tank, high-pressure electric fuel pump, fuel pressure regulator, and numerous fittings for the supply and return lines. I will do my best to make these modern parts hide in plain sight by stripping off any colored anodized finish and using black woven hose in place of braided hoses.

Electrical

I will keep everything simple but must retain all lights and gauges as well as supply power to the various EFI components and engine management equipment. The GMPP ZZ502/502 deluxe kit comes with an HEI distributor, starter, and plug wires—use 'em. To trigger it all, use an MSD 6A-L.

Funny Stuff

These are the detail items that will further enhance the funny car theme and put the car over the top.

Try to include a reproduction Mopar Super Stock battery in the trunk. Again, these things were sold over the counter in the 1960s and many appeared in the trunks of non-Mopar match race cars as an excellent way to add nearly 100 pounds of ballast over the driving wheels.

A silver parachute pack on the trunk or rear bumper is a must to complete the funny car vibrations. It is a lot of work packing a 'chute after every pass, plus with the front disc brakes and sub-130-mph trap speeds, the chute would rarely, if ever, be needed. Maybe a dummy would suffice?

Super critical is some sort of wheelie wheel or a set of wheelie bars. Keep it simple, a bit crude even, just like they were. A single wheelbarrow wheel hanging beneath the center of the rear bumper would be super kinky. Beswick used one on his 1966 GTO. Or, if a set of casters are chosen, have them hang down from a pair of upside-down leaf springs with the ends bent at a 45-degree angle. Either way, these things will probably have to be

CHAPTER 2

functional. Remember, if the nose comes up suddenly, the wheelie wheels will eventually contact the strip. Do you want the load transferred into the rear axle and suspension? Or do you want the load transferred into the body of the car where a distinct beam load (bending) will be imposed on the quarter panels? I'd go for the suspension mount to minimize the likelihood of bodywork damage! Think this over and by all means, design every aspect of the car to avoid the damage caused by bumper-dragging wheelies!

Another major detail—and a potential way to tame wheelies—is the addition of a small Moon tank hanging off the front of the car. This doesn't have to be a functional component of the fuel system; in fact, it is best left empty of any flammable liquids. The alternate role for the Moon tank could be as a ballast container. That's right, if filled with lead shot, it could add as much as 50 to 75 pounds to the prow of the ship. That could go a long way toward keeping the front end closer to the track. Make sure the mounting system is up to the task of securing a fully laden Moon tank amid the bounces and jolts of street and strip combat!

A great opportunity to score even more funny points is to build a large aluminum chin spoiler and hang it beneath the front bumper. It was a common sight as speeds went over 150 mph and racers sought ways to prevent their cars from going airborne in the traps. Such a spoiler also provides an excellent opportunity for a fun logo or other painted treatment. Butch Leal's *California Flash* altered wheelbase 1965 Plymouth wore an odd cartoon of a dog chasing a scalded ape on its chin spoiler. Have some fun!

Further aerodynamic tailoring can be performed by adding a stand-up lip spoiler to the trailing edge of the trunk lid. Again, such aero appendages began to sprout as the funnies switched to alky and nitro and shattered the 150-mph barrier.

Taking a page from NASCAR stock car competition, some funny car racers placed backlight retainer straps over the rear window to keep it in place at top speed. Likely only applicable to situations where plexiglass windows were used, it would be redundant on my Nova with its stock rubber gasket and flange retainer design. It would still look cool though….

Remember that the above was written months before any work was begun on the 1963 Nova that eventually became the *Wilshire Shaker*. Follow along now, as the photographs and captions below describe the actual construction process. Pay attention to see which ideas and features from the "recipe list" made the cut, and which ones didn't.

Plan and Prepare for Surgery

Purchased on November 8, 1997, for $750, the 1963 Nova still wore much of its original green paint and was virtually rust free. Always buy the cleanest car you can; it'll make merging the metal after surgery much easier than adding the burden of repairing rust damage and accident tweaks.

WILSHIRE SHAKER NOVA CONSTRUCTION OVERVIEW

You can sell unneeded parts to help finance the project. We sold the front fenders, hood, and bumper for $225; the air-cooled Powerglide and 250-cube six-banger went for $100. This dropped the net vehicle purchase price to $425.

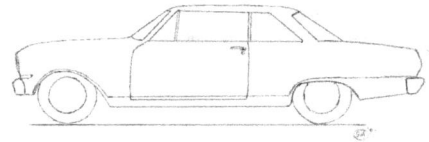

To help visualize wheelbase alteration options, take a photo of the side of the car and then trace over it with a pencil. This one depicts the Nova prior to wheelbase modification and serves as a jumping-off point.

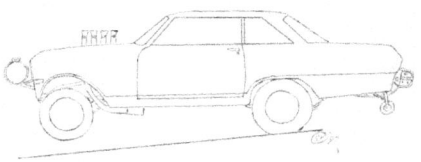

Using an eraser and pencil you can adjust the wheelbase and work out different induction, suspension, header, and bodywork strategies before making the final commitment in metal. In this drawing the front and rear wheel openings have been moved forward in the fashion of the 1965 Chrysler FX fleet cars. Note the nearly stock rear wheel opening. This strategy calls for delicate sectioning of the lower rear quarter panels to retain the stock contour. Increased ride height is an essential Match Bash feature. Note that the body is raised so the bottom edge of the rocker panel is in line with the wheel spindles. Stance is everything.

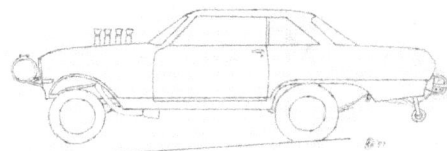

This drawing represents a more raw approach to the rear wheel opening. Rather than fuss with awkward patching behind the wheel opening, a simple stretch in the middle does the job and is a treatment used on many period match racers including Dyno Don Nicholson's 1965 SOHC Cyclone. The repositioned front wheel opening shown didn't materialize since the curves and contours of the stock Nova front fenders are quite complex and would have been difficult to manipulate. Instead, some basic tire clearance trimming was performed with tin snips to make room for the 4-inch-forward relocation of the front axle centerline.

Wilshire Shaker in Miniature

"Hello, Steve. My name is Hollie Holmes. I'm with Mattel and I handle licensing and acquisitions agreements for our vehicles group. I'm looking to chat with you because our design team has identified your *Wilshire Shaker* as a car that they would like to potentially replicate for our Hot Wheels collector line. Please give me a call soon so we can discuss this matter."

That's the message I found on my answering machine one evening.

At first I thought it was a prank but Ms. Holmes' voice sounded too sincere. Totally excited at the prospect of having one of my cars rendered in miniature—by Hot Wheels, no less—I returned her call early the next morning. Her first concern was whether the *Wilshire Shaker* was a replica of an actual car or if I thought it up myself. I told her all about how it riffs on the original line of *Seaton's Shaker* match racers but I had inserted the word *Wilshire* in reference to the address of *Hot Rod* magazine—where I worked at the time. As far as I knew, there was no trademark on the name and no reason why we couldn't do the model.

She asked me to shoot numerous detail pictures of the car so the Mattel designers could further evaluate the feasibility of doing a 1/64-scale replica. The photos would also be used to help the Mattel legal affairs people check the various sponsor logos and graphic elements on the body for potential complications.

A few weeks later, Hollie called to say the car passed all legal tests and Hot Wheels wanted to move forward with a palm-size die-cast replica. As payment I had the choice of a flat fee of $1,200 or no money and 300 of the Hot Wheels miniatures. I split the offer and requested $600 and 150 cars so I'd get some cash but also have lots of *Wilshire Shaker* replicas to hand out to friends and family in the coming years. We had a deal.

About five months later two boxes arrived at my doorstep, directly from Mattel's Bangkok, Thailand, manufacturing plant. Inside were 150 little *Wilshire Shakers*. Part of the Hot Wheels Drag Strip Demons line of nostalgia-themed 1/64 die-cast models, the Nova is number 13 in a series that includes replicas of the *Beebe & Mulligan* fuel dragster, Dave Strickler's *Dodge Boys* altered wheelbase 1965 Dodge, Sox & Martin's 1968 SS/B Hemi Barracuda, Roland Leong's *Hawaiian* Charger funny car, and several other famous cars from the golden age of drag racing. Heady company indeed; I was deeply honored.

The execution of the model is very good, though the change from "It's a 502 Semi-Hemi" to "It's a 502" on the front fenders hints that Mattel might have to pay a royalty to Chrysler for use of the H-word. Also, the Cragar and Art Carr logos are missing from the model, likely for similar reasons. Perhaps the best development is that Hot Wheels now has an altered wheelbase 1963 Nova tooling, so we can probably look forward to future releases with different markings. If they do a replica of the Steve Bovan *Blair's Speed Shop* supercharged match racer, I'm a customer!

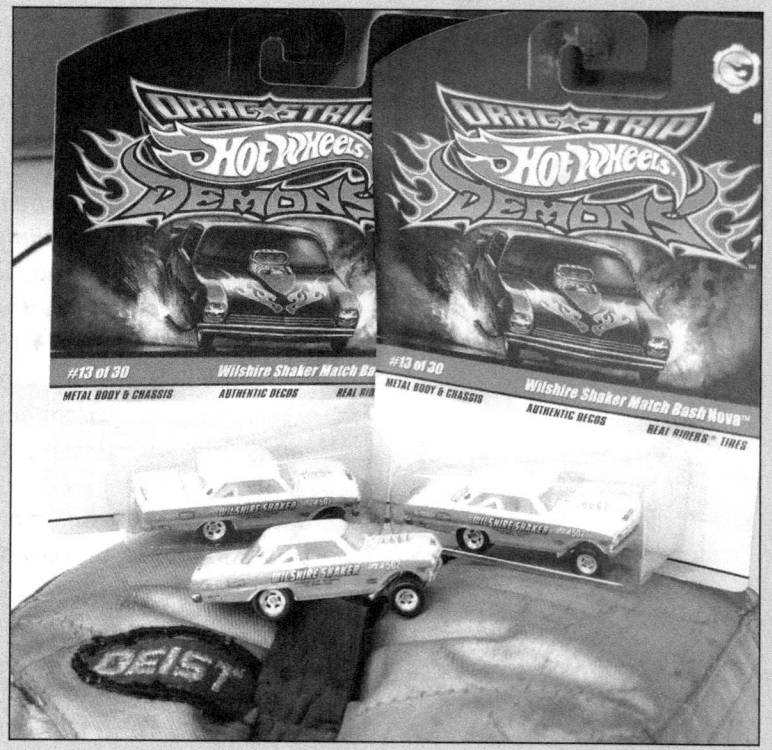

Move the Rear Wheels

After studying the drawings, Phil Mandella and Larry Zavala (foreground) measure the stock 110-inch wheelbase prior to surgery. Phil's approach to rear wheel relocation involves complete rear axle and leaf spring removal prior to cutting. Several jack stands support the body to prevent sagging and flex.

Using a plasma cutter and reciprocating electric saw, Phil cuts the entire rear floorpan and axle hump out of the car. Though some of the other altered wheelbase conversion work shown in other sections of this book keeps the rear suspension and wheels intact as a unit during surgery, in Phil's opinion these bulky components complicate the process.

After the perimeter cut is made, the rear floorpan drops to the ground. Note that the stock wheel housings are still in place in this shot. On this project, Phil elected to attack the Nova's inner structure before turning his attention to the external body panels.

Here's the rear axle hump after being moved forward 10 inches and tack welded in position. While the stock wheel houses could be mini-tubbed for added tire clearance, it is a time-consuming operation.

Instead, a Competition Engineering steel wheel tub kit (PN C3003) is trimmed to fit and welded into place. With retro looks, they easily clear the 29-inch-tall Mickey Thompson/Radir 15x10-inch nostalgia slicks. Because the relocated wheel tubs occupy the same space as the rear side windows, they must be installed in a permanently raised position using metal tabs and screws. And naturally, the rear seat is a thing of the past.

Rectangular 2 x 4-inch steel tubing is welded in place to bridge the gap between the stock Nova frame segments after stretching. The end result is stronger than the stock configuration.

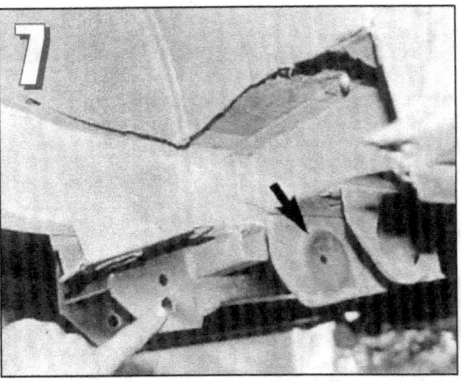

Early Nova racers have always suffered with awkward stock leaf-spring positioning that limits tire width. Phil sidesteps the problem by using Competition Engineering weld-in sub-frame connectors (PN C3047) that reposition the leaf springs inboard and allow plenty of sidewall clearance. Here, my finger points to the new leaf-spring mount and the arrow points out the original Nova location.

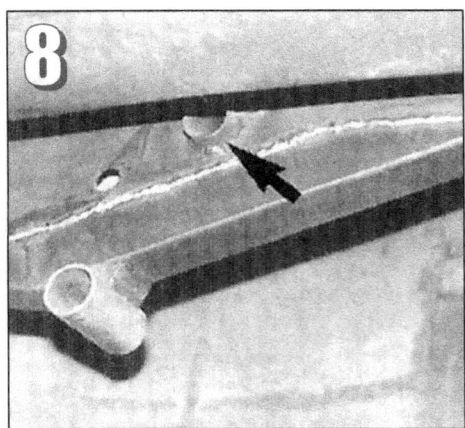

The longitudinal frame rails beneath the trunk floor are unmodified except for add-on spacers (outlined in chalk for clarity). The circular tube (arrow) was the initial rear shackle location that failed to yield the desired ride height, thus the welded steel extensions.

The 1964 Mercury Park Lane 9-inch housing features a 4.56:1 gear ratio and a Detroit Locker unit from Currie Enterprises. The housing is narrowed to measure 56 inches drum-to-drum, so the slicks sit just right in the wheel openings with the 4.25-inch backspacing of the Cragar 15 x 7-inch S/S mag wheels. Mopar Performance 3,800-pound Super Stock leaf springs (PN 3690454/455) and extra-travel drag shocks (PN 4529515) don't discriminate between vehicle makes; they work under anything. Thanks to the inboard location of the front spring mounts, the leaf springs splay outward to meet the rear shackles. The welded axle mounts are oriented straight ahead and the U-bolts clamp everything together.

With the inner structure moved forward 10 inches and welded in its final position, Phil moves outside the car and uses the saw to cut 10-inch-long sections out of the quarter-panel skin. The top of the wheel opening is also trimmed free of the body so it can be moved forward to fill the gap. All cuts must be made straight and level to avoid misalignment during reassembly.

WILSHIRE SHAKER NOVA CONSTRUCTION OVERVIEW

Here Phil slides the loose wheel opening section forward to model its final position prior to welding. Notice how this strategy minimizes the size of the needed patch, greatly simplifying the process, and reducing the amount of bodywork while delivering period-correct Match Bash results.

After tack welding the segment in place, the stretched wheel opening begins to take shape. Again, clean, straight cuts minimize the amount of patching needed and reduce the chance of misaligned body lines and botched contours. The Chrysler 15 x 7-inch steel rims are temporary rollers.

With the major portion of Phil Mandella's rear axle relocation work completed, the car is ready for fabricator Dale Kutch to replace the clunky stock front suspension and bolt-on frame with a replica of the Bill Thomas Instant Funny Car Nova tubular frame kit from 1966. Bill Thomas ran a California Chevrolet dealership and was heavily involved in many forms of racing. His Instant Funny Car tubular front clip was used on many Chevy II match racers including Dick Harrell's *Retribution II*. Bill Thomas was also responsible for the legendary Cheetah sports car, built to take on Shelby's Cobras.

Before tackling the front clip, Dale welded in some metal patches and did the preliminary bodywork to smooth the surgery scars. The black primer prevents rust.

HOW TO BUILD ALTERED WHEELBASE CARS

CHAPTER 2

Replace the Front Subframe

After stripping away the stock front suspension items, the bare front clip was sold for $50 to a 1965 Nova owner who'd just had an accident and needed a replacement. This dropped our Nova's net buy-in price to $375.

Chevrolet engineers did Nova funny car builders a huge favor by designing the car with a removable front clip that's attached to the cowl by 14 bolts. Weighing 289 pounds fully dressed, the stock clip has intrusive spring towers and crossmembers that complicate big-block engine swaps. It's a dead player for Match Bash use.

Using vintage photographs from the March 1966 issue of Hot Rod magazine, Dale copied the Bill Thomas Instant Funny Car front clip using 2-inch-diameter main tubes with 1.50-inch tubes for everything else. All tubing is .120-inch-thick mild steel. To ease muscle strain during the fabrication of the motor mounts, he used a full-size plastic Chevy big-block mock-up model from P-Ayr Products.

Prepare the Engine and Transmission

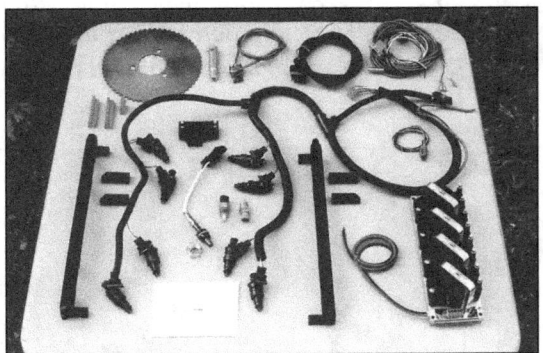

While Dale gets the front suspension set up, the GMPP ZZ502/502 deluxe engine kit is uncrated for assembly and conversion to funny car status. When altered wheelbase Chevy funny cars first rose up against the Mopar Hemis in 1965, some used 409 and 427 Z-11 power, but the new-for-1965 Rat proved to be the most effective weapon. We're celebrating that fact with this modern 502, but it'll get the retro touch.

The crate engines' cast-aluminum valve covers are too modern and dilute the retro vibe, so a set of traditional smooth valve covers from a 1995 Suburban were fitted with welded-on tall breather tubes (a la Arnie Beswick's 421 GTO) for extra Match Bash vibrations. The entire engine was stripped of the factory-issue black paint and covered in several coats of Chevrolet Orange Red from OEM Paints (PN 62020).

By 1966, competitive 1960s match racers ran either individual-runner mechanical fuel injection or a Roots blower. Carburetors were for also-rans. Knowing this, we substituted the ZZ502's cast-aluminum single-quad intake manifold and 850-cfm Holley for an Electromotive Tec-III engine controller that runs the Hilborn C-396E EFI induction system with 55-lb/hr injectors. Taking cues from throttle position, air inlet temperature, and crankshaft position sensors, the Tec-III delivers excellent power while maintaining street manners that users of mechanical fuel injection can only dream about. Remember, Match Bash is all about street as well as strip.

With no other changes, the Hilborn/Electromotive individual-runner EFI raised power output from the stock rating of 502 hp at 5,200 rpm to 528 hp at 5,000 rpm and 567 ft-lbs at 4,200 rpm to 607 ft-lbs at 3,500 rpm. That's a 26- and 40-ft-lb gain, respectively—plus a huge boost in eye appeal and Match Bash credibility. Using a simple magnetic crank trigger and remote coil packs, the ZZ502's Delco HEI distributor is no longer needed. Best of all, the 9.8:1 compression ratio runs great on 91-octane unleaded gas.

CHAPTER 2

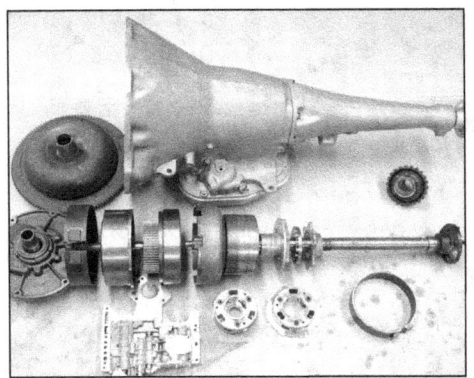

The only modern automatic transmission available to match racers prior to 1966 was the cable-operated 1962–1965 Chrysler 727 Torqueflite. Study early magazine photos and you'll see push-button Torqueflites in Chevys and Fords until 1967 when Turbo 400s and Police-spec C6s finally arrived on the scene. To capture the dial-a-win vibe, we sent this 1964 318 Belvedere transmission to Art Carr for fortification. It's got a reverse-pattern full-manual valve body, beefed clutches and bands, and a 1968-up input shaft and pump so a modern 3,000-rpm-stall-speed torque converter can be used. The transmission and converter weigh 173 pounds dry. A pre-1965 Chrysler ball-and-trunion driveshaft was shortened to 33.75 inches to compensate for the 10-inch rear axle relocation.

A Wilcap adapter and B&M Chrysler flexplate (PN 10230) completes the unholy union between the Chrysler Torqueflite and Chevy Rat motor. Though vintage B&M, Art Carr and C&O Torqueflite adapters mandate a big-block (361-426-style) 727, the Wilcap kit calls for a small-block (318-style) transmission, which is good news because big-block push-button Torqueflites are highly prized among restorers and racers while small-block variants are dumpster bait. If you see a bell housing bolt hole at the 12 o'clock position, it's a big-block case. Liquid threadlocking compound must be used on all fasteners to prevent loosening.

A 1964 Dodge D100 pickup truck donated its push-button shift pod. Mounted to the Nova's dash, the Art Carr full-manual-valve body changes gears with the push of a button. A push-pull cable connects the shift unit to the Torqueflite. If you want push buttons in your Match Bash creation, you'll need a 1962–1965 727 Torqueflite. Later units switched to lever-operation and do not accept push-button controls.

When he wasn't running his 8-second, 165-mph Chevy 2 Much Nova altered wheelbase funny car, match race legend Doug Thorley ran a highly successful header business. Though recently retired, Doug built the Wilshire Shaker's cool bundle-of-snakes headers. The collectors are fitted with 3-inch bolt-on caps that can be uncorked at the drag strip.

WILSHIRE SHAKER NOVA CONSTRUCTION OVERVIEW

During the gestation period, the car was mocked up several times to check progress. Here it sits after chassis completion but before bodywork. The ill-fitting fiberglass front fenders shown were replaced by steel reproductions from Goodmark. Some observers said the car should have been left this way, super raw and very mean looking. It's a valid sentiment that influenced the construction of the Rampage Dart featured elsewhere in this book.

Paint and Bodywork

1 After delivery to Spray-Rite Auto Body in Monrovia, all surgery scars have been healed and the car wears a coat of black guide-coat paint. The guys were chirping again that it should be left this way. No dice; the full Match Bash effect can only be achieved with period-inspired paint and graphics. Surprisingly, the Goodmark steel reproduction front fenders (PN 4010-100-62-L/R) weigh only 2 pounds more than the thick fiberglass copies. Either medium is fair game for Match Bash use today, though most period cars relied on fiberglass replacement fenders, hoods, bumpers, trunk lids, and doors to shed weight.

Deciding exactly what paint and graphics treatment to apply is a major decision for modern Match Bash builders. Avoid copycat treatments of famous cars unless you've got the real thing—and written permission. These fanciful renderings are a trial run to get the creative juices flowing.

HOW TO BUILD ALTERED WHEELBASE CARS

Vintage drag racing magazines are a valuable asset and yield plenty of great ideas. We settled on an orange-and-white two-tone treatment as a tribute to Pete Seaton's series of Chevelle, Corvair, and Nova match racers. Though Seaton never campaigned a first-generation Nova, the two-tone treatment looks great on ours.

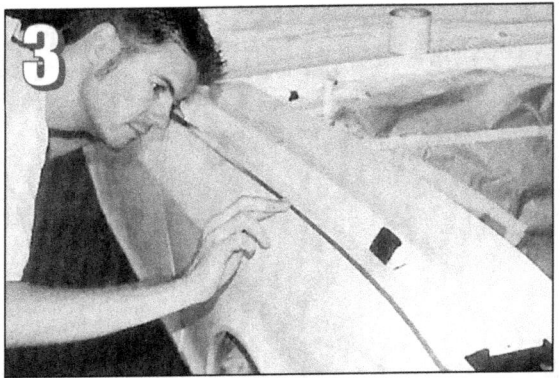

When it comes to two-tone paint schemes, always apply the lightest color first. Spray-Rite Auto Body applied the PPG DMD663 White first, then Jamie Seymour, a graduate of the Art Center College of Design in Pasadena, masked the body in preparation for the PPG 60156 Tangier Orange secondary color.

After wet sanding and application of PPG 2010 Clear coat, the Nova blossoms into a thing of beauty. The border between the orange and white colors was applied high on the Nova's flanks to give plenty of room for the graphic treatment.

The six-point roll bar is coated with Rust-Oleum Smoke Gray brush paint. That's right, brush paint. After it dries for a week, the oil-based enamel is wet sanded to a mirror-smooth finish that's almost as tough as powder coating and far more scratch-resistant than spray paint.

The firewall and cowl are finished in semi-gloss enamel to serve as an excellent contrasting backdrop for the bright orange Rat motor. The hole for the heater motor on the passenger side of the firewall has been patch welded and finished for a smooth appearance to make the Nova look like an original heater delete car.

Install Front Clip and Straight Axle

Specialty Cars supplied a tube steel straight axle that delivers a not-too-wide, not-too-narrow 56.5-inch front track width (48 inches kingpin-to-kingpin). The Wilwood disc brakes mount to reproduction 1937–1941 Ford spindles from Total Cost Involved (TCI). The four-leaf front springs are from Eaton Detroit Spring and are rated at 1,500 pounds each. At 34 inches eye-to-eye and with a 6-inch arch (unloaded), they offer a great balance of sustained ride height and the ability to handle bumps, potholes, and wheelies without trouble.

After being coated with Rust-Oleum Smoke Gray enamel, then wet sanded, the completed tubular front clip is bolted in place. The front axle and springs wear a coat of Rust-Oleum Gloss Black (also applied with a brush, then wet sanded.)

Wilwood heavy-duty vented front disc brakes (PN 140-2260) weigh 28 pounds and mount to TCI reproduction 1937–1941 Ford spindles. Though most period match racers didn't employ front brakes for low weight, they're essential for street use. Gabriel 1/2-ton Chevy pickup truck gas shocks (PN 737923) dampen road irregularities.

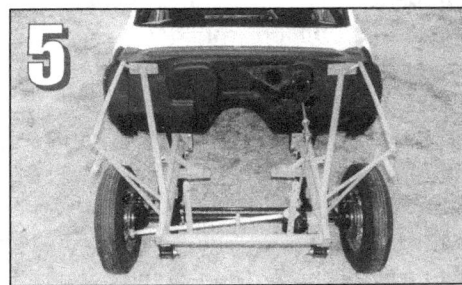

In keeping with the original Bill Thomas Instant Funny Car kit, the front axle centerline is moved forward 4 inches, bringing the wheelbase to 104 inches (110 is stock). The overall length of the lower main frame tubes is 37½ inches and the total width is 32¾ inches. The distance between the leaf-spring mounting bolt holes is 32¼ inches. A Flaming River steering box bolts to the frame and a custom 3/4-inch steering column takes inputs from the Moon steering wheel.

Another view of the front clip shows the elegant simplicity of the Bill Thomas design. The entire clip (less wheels and tires) weighs 226 pounds, complete with brakes and steering box. The slender outriggers support the Goodmark Industries reproduction steel fenders. Before the arrival of lightweight 1,600-pound flip-top funny cars—which used small front tires—most door-slammer Match Bash cars weighed at least 2,400 pounds and needed beefy front tires. To get the look, we sourced reproduction BF Goodrich Silvertown 6.40-15-inch bias-ply front tires from Coker. They're 26.8 inches in diameter, have delicate 4.20-inch treads, and are perfect. They mount to 15 x 4.5-inch Cragar S/S wheels. Though modern radial tires may handle better; they just look wrong.

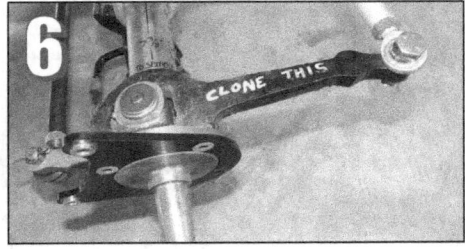

The passenger-side spindle takes steering inputs from the steering box and cross-steer drag link via this fabricated 3/4-inch-thick steel steering arm. Cross-steering is superior to near-steering (where the steering box is linked to the driver-side front wheel) because the length of the drag link—which spans from the steering box to the passenger-side front wheel—dampens the transmission of road shocks and suspension undulations into the steering wheel. Cars with cross-steering tend to require minimal driver corrections to stay on course, while near-steer designs keep the driver on his toes as the car darts around with every road bump.

CHAPTER 2

Apply Graphics and Install Engine

Though the original Seaton's Shaker was a Chevelle, the tasteful two-tone paint scheme works just as well on the smaller Nova. Bob Thompson handled all the graphics and applies 22-carat deep-gold-leaf lettering and hand-brushed sponsor logos. Gold leaf comes in $3\frac{3}{8}$ x $3\frac{3}{8}$-inch-square sheets and disintegrates in your hands if you're rough with it. About $98 worth was used to letter both sides of the car. Brushed-on clear lacquer seals the gold foil after thumb-swirls are made with a velvet cloth.

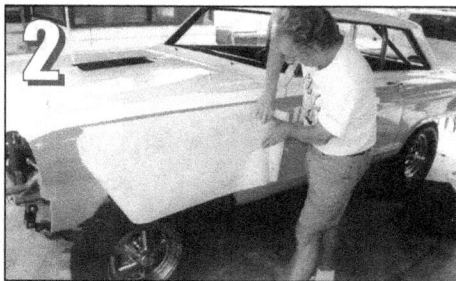

Professional results call for identical lettering and art on both sides of the car. To get it, Bob traces the design onto a sheet of paper and then uses a ponce wheel to make perforations in the paper along the traced pencil lines. Then, the paper is taped to the opposite side of the car and chalk powder is applied. This gives Bob an exact outline of where to apply his brush strokes so a mirror image is created. Until the late 1960s, the vast majority of match racers featured hand-brushed lettering. Air brushing didn't take root until the arrival of damage-prone flip-top funny cars in the late 1960s.

Decked out in orange paint and fitted with Hilborn injection, the 502 Rat looks like it was just pulled out of Dave Strickler's stretched 1966 Corvette match racer. Though some might choose to polish the aluminum parts and add chrome dress-up details, when it comes to Match Bash cars, less is usually more.

The injector stacks are removed to prevent damage during engine installation. Fabricator Dale Kutsch fitted the front clip with rugged engine mounts that work with stock urethane isolators from Energy Suspension (PN 3-1114) to keep the torquey 502 anchored.

Here's a look at the cross-steering arrangement with the engine in place. Heim swivel joints on each end of the drag link prevent binding and allow for fine adjustment. The steering tie rod is set to deliver 3/16 inch of toe-in.

The fast-ratio Flaming River 16:1 GM A-body manual steering box feeds driver inputs to the steering link via a forged-steel pitman arm. Notice the 1-inch spacer sleeve and extra-length through-bolt used on the small end. These details were added to drop the steering link since it was making occasional contact with the spinning harmonic damper during suspension compression on heavy dips in the road. Now the problem is solved with no ill effects on steering geometry. All fasteners are Grade 8, and Nylock nuts or lock washers are used throughout to prevent loosening.

WILSHIRE SHAKER NOVA CONSTRUCTION OVERVIEW

The Electromotive Tec-III employs a crank trigger and external coil packs to fire the spark plugs, so the traditional ignition distributor is eliminated. The MSD 8.8-mm wires route into the car through an insulated plastic body plug to meet the under-dash Electromotive coil pack. A Mallory dummy distributor fills the vacant distributor-location hole in the intake manifold and runs the oil pump.

Under the dash, a custom bracket locates the Tec-III unit where it's nice and cool. Tuning is accomplished via a laptop computer. The integral coil packs fire the spark plugs.

Ford-sourced aluminum A/FX radiators were highly sought after by weight-conscious match racers back in the day. To capture the vibe on our modern Match Bash tribute, Griffin built a 17-inch aluminum replica. It may look small but its high-efficiency 3-inch core keeps the Rat cool. A Spal 16-inch electric fan (PN VA18-AP6-41MA) kicks in at low vehicle speed; there's no room for an engine-driven mechanical fan.

The stock GMPP aluminum water pump is driven by reproduction deep-groove L-88 pulleys from Big Block Supply. A Moroso filler neck (PN 63420) joins the coolant fittings on the Hilborn intake manifold to the upper radiator hose. A Powermaster 100-amp alternator keeps the trunk-mounted battery charged. The absence of chromed and polished surfaces gives the engine bay a no-nonsense Match Bash vibe.

Mufflers are a must for street operation so Bassani whipped up this stainless steel X-pipe with quad outlet mufflers. It connects to outlets welded into the custom Doug Thorley fenderwell headers. The exhaust system is designed to tuck up against the floor so it is nearly invisible when the Nova is viewed from the side and rear. Low-hanging mufflers spoil the race-only illusion.

Interior Details

Though most match racers used lightweight plastic windows all around, Match Bash cars are meant for street cruising so a glass windshield must be used for safety. We also retained the glass backlight (though plastic would be an acceptable substitute). Brand-new reproduction window glass is available for virtually all popular Match Bash vehicle candidates.

Vintage photos of match racers show that most builders eliminated the door vent windows and substituted the door glass with a one-piece plastic replica. To remain true, we made cardboard templates and cut our door windows from Lexan sheet. The stock Nova window top frame and support are then attached to the new windows using press-fit rubber sheets made for this purpose. Most auto glass supply houses carry it.

When the stock door vent windows are eliminated, the forward window-lift tracks and regulators are also lost. We retained the rearmost window-lift tracks and fabricated a custom forward track so the door glass can still be raised and lowered.

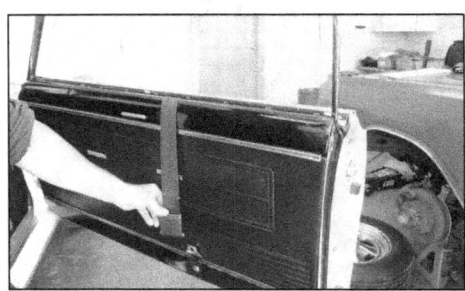

Based on a 1970 Plymouth Duster seatbelt-and-buckle assembly, each door window can be raised and lowered by simply pulling the straps. The buckle clicks into a tab secured to the bottom of the door to hold the windows in the raised position for racing. The beauty of Classic Industries reproduction vinyl door panels (PN N61301) is their lack of holes for door latches and window regulators. You're supposed to punch these areas out prior to installation. This is a happy accident for us. We left them un-punched for a nice finished look.

The rear side windows were also duplicated in Lexan using the stock glass as a pattern. Once completed, small tabs of aluminum angle stock are screwed to the windows and rest on the window sill to keep the panels in the permanently raised position. All window frames are fitted with fresh rubber weather stripping from Steele Rubber Products so the cabin is relatively weather tight.

Since the rear axle has been moved forward 10 inches and large wheel tubs have invaded the interior, the stock interior panels no longer fit. But, they can be trimmed to suit the new arrangement. The cardboard pattern was made to fit the revised wheel tubs then was used to guide the cutting of the reproduction panels from Classic Industries (PN N63801).

On the Cover of *Hot Rod* Magazine

Okay this is cheating a little bit since I was a staff member, but doesn't everybody dream of getting their car on the cover of *Hot Rod*? Well it's not as easy as just being an employee. The car has to merit the attention. So when then-editor and former *Super Stock & Drag Illustrated* staffer Ro McGonegal said he wanted to use the car on the cover of the May 2001 issue, I said, "Ro, it's nowhere near finished!" He said not to worry, so I quickly mocked the car together—wearing temporary black guide coat, and trailered it over to the *Hot Rod* Van Nuys project garage. There, photographer James Brown immortalized the car during an afternoon-long photo session on February 1, 2001.

To spice it up, I borrowed a vintage silver fuel suit and Bell open-face helmet from Jim and Marion Deist. Looking like a space man, Brown had me pose with the car to add a vintage mood to the shots. For the most part I was just standing there until he suggested I jump inside the car and poke up through the empty windshield opening. We were just being goofy at first but the shots turned out better than expected and Ro selected one for the cover.

My only regret is the car wasn't yet painted with its distinctive two-tone treatment and snazzy gold-leaf lettering. But those details wouldn't be finished for another three years! The hectic nature of being technical editor at *Hot Rod* meant a never-ending stream of deadlines and constant writing. I had very little time to work on the Nova so its construction took an agonizing six years. By contrast, I got the *Rampage* Dart and *Funny Fairmont* each done within a year! Of course by then I had left *Hot Rod* for a freelance writing career so I had more time to work on the cars.

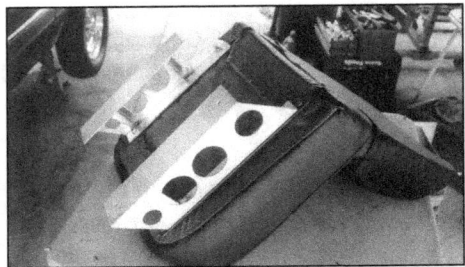

Bench seats are not correct for Match Bash cars. You need buckets, but steer clear of modern high-back designs since they destroy the illusion. The best choice is a set of Dodge A100 seats resting on reproduction Race Hemi seat brackets from Kramer Automotive Specialties. Late Chevy match race legend Richard Schroeder's Bad Bossa Nova *used a single Dodge bucket seat, as did all of the 1965 Mopar factory A/FX fleet.*

Many original match racers featured completely gutted interiors but others were less austere. With its vinyl-covered interior panels and black carpet, our Nova takes the middle road. We eliminated the headliner and sprayed all exposed surfaces with Zolotone trunk spatter paint from Eastwood. Notice the window-lift strap and trim-to-fit wheel tub surrounds. The rear side windows are held up by small aluminum tabs and screws.

CHAPTER 2

Fuel System and Loose Ends

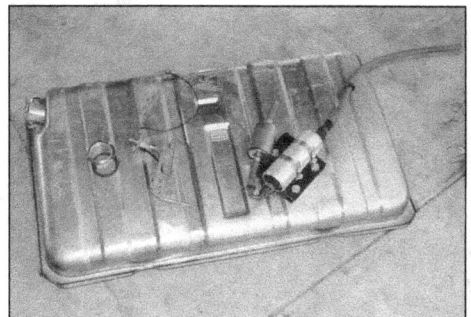

For plenty of range during street excursions, we installed a 16-gallon reproduction 1962–1967 Nova gas tank from Classic Industries. It mounts in the stock location, but since the stock external fuel-fill cap was welded shut for aesthetics, the filler neck has been moved inside the trunk compartment. A fully welded steel panel divides the trunk from the interior for safety. The electric fuel pump is an externally mounted Accel inline unit that feeds the 3/8-inch supply and return lines with ease.

When altered wheelbase match racers started running alcohol and nitromethane fuel mixtures, small external fuel tanks, such as this 5-gallon item, from Moon were often mounted on the front bumper. In the case of our pump-gas-fed Nova, the tank remains dry and is not part of the fuel system. But it's no bogus decoration and was mounted on a beefy support so up to 50 pounds of lead shot can be added to curb wheelies.

The Currie 11 x 3-inch drum brakes (PN CE6005-A) work well with Wilwood front disc brakes to deliver plenty of fade-free stopping power. The Currie 31-spline axle shafts are far stronger than the 28-spline axles used in basic Ford 9-inch axles and easily withstand full-throttle wheels-up launches at the strip.

The narrowed rear axle (56 inches drum-to-drum), generous wheel tubs, and increased ride height offer lots of sidewall clearance.

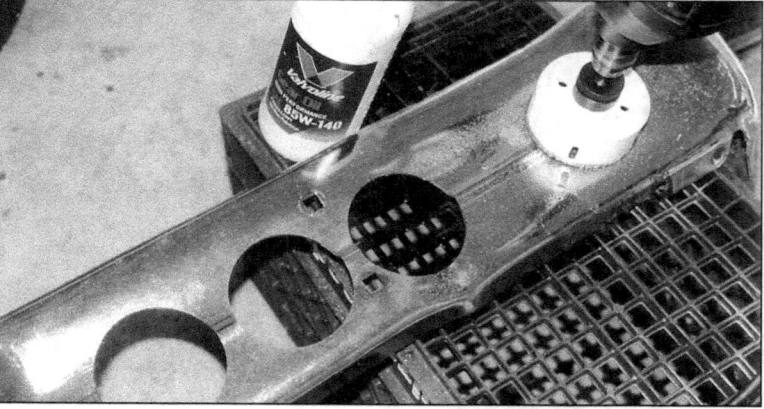

Small details add up and one classic Match Bash feature is the "Swiss cheese" bumper treatment. It starts with careful measuring to ensure symmetrical results, then a 3-inch hole saw is used to make the cuts. A steady flow of gear lube extends the life of the saw, though ours was about used up after we finished the eighth hole.

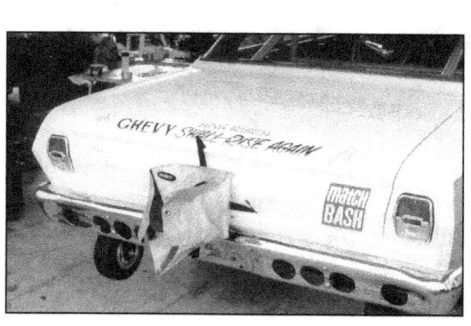

Once the holes were cut, the bumper was sent out for re-chroming. Another classic Match Bash feature is a parachute. Ours is strictly decorative—the wheel brakes are more than enough for the Shaker's low 11-second/130-mph potential—so we stuffed it full of old T-shirts.

WILSHIRE SHAKER NOVA CONSTRUCTION OVERVIEW

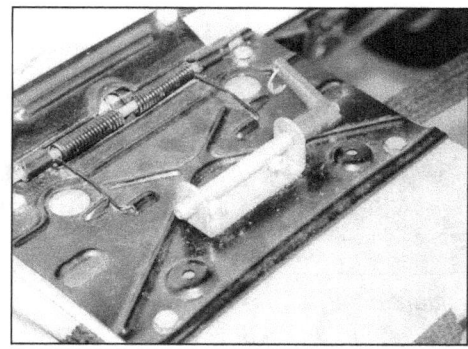

The parachute bag is mounted to an aluminum backing plate that's bolted to a recycled folding license plate hinge. Just push the button on the latch and the 'chute folds down for trunk-key access. Mounting the dummy parachute lower would have obscured the rear license plate, a no-no on street-driven Match Bash cars.

Up front, a 48 x 15-inch cardboard pattern was made to help determine the size of the front spoiler. Truth be told, such aerodynamic aids are not necessary until you enter the 140-mph zone, but the look is irresistible. Steel rear bumpers are A-OK but proper Match Bashers should use a lightweight fiberglass replica up front. Ours is from Unlimited Fiberglass and wears a coat of silver spray paint.

The final spoiler depth is 9 inches, not too big and not too small. Glistens Custom Metal Polishing added the engine-turned effect and Bob Thompson applied the groovy 502 Much logo. Sturdy metal brackets attach the spoiler to the frame.

The trunk compartment and roll-bar down tubes were given a heavy coat of Rust-Oleum Smoke Gray brush paint. After it dried for a week, Eastwood Zolotone spatter paint was applied for a quasi-factory stock appearance. The steel battery tray on the right accommodates a reproduction Mopar Super Stock battery from Kramer Automotive Specialties. At 100 pounds wet, it's a classic Match Bash touch that helps plant the slicks for extra traction. Stay away from trunk-mounted plastic fuel cells for Match Bash use; they're just too "modern."

Many match racers were based on rejuvenated factory super stock vehicles and low-line strippers—most of which were built without the unnecessary expense of a radio. I searched long and hard for a correct radio delete plate. It came from an ad in Hemmings Motor News and cost $100, a small price to pay for the interior's crowning touch. Dig the cool Moon steering wheel. The metal-flake-orange vinyl grip compliments the Shaker's two-tone paint scheme.

CHAPTER 2

Test and Tune

The finished car weighs 3,040 pounds with a full tank of gas. A four-wheel scale session shows that the front tires carry 1,392 pounds and the rear slicks carry 1,648 pounds. That's a 45.8/54.2 front/rear static weight distribution—proof positive the altered wheelbase surgery yields tangible real-world results.

Initial testing at the Irwindale 1/8-mile strip resulted in a best run of 7.674 seconds at 90.29 mph with an impressive 1.779-second 60-foot time. Not bad, but the 502 refused to pull beyond 6,000 rpm. So we swapped the ZZ502/502 0.527/0.544 lift, 224/234 duration hydraulic roller cam with a hotter solid roller from Crane. With .615/.636 lift and 246/254 duration, the Crane replacement (PN 168601) improved breathing and now the engine spins all the way to 7,000 rpm without strain. (Mike Morgan)

To get the most from the Electromotive electronic engine management system, we took the car to DynoWorks where Joe Morgan used the chassis dyno to fine-tune the calibrations. A bit of tweaking delivered 346 hp and 486 ft-lbs of torque to the tires. Fuel economy is just over 10 mpg, not a bad figure considering the 4.56:1 rear axle ratio and high-stall torque converter. The STP stickers applied to the headlamps are a nod to the effect seen in vintage photos of Shirley Shahan's *Drag-On Lady* 1965 Plymouth match racer.

We haven't tested the new cam on the chassis dyno but immediate improvements—and wheelies—resulted at the track. A second trip to Irwindale delivered a string of 7.2- and 7.1-second passes at 92 and 93 mph, respectively. Uncorking the headers and bypassing the mufflers produced a surprising 6.960-second pass at 95.94 mph with a 2-foot wheelie and 1.482-second 60-foot time. Using the NHRA 1/8- to 1/4-mile-conversion factor (ET x 1.57), that 6.9-second pass is like a 10.92 and the muffled runs suggest low-11-second performance in the full quarter-mile. Thanks to the 46/54 front/rear static weight distribution, made possible by the wheelbase relocation surgery, the rock-hard M/T-Radir nostalgia drag slicks hook like glue with no spin whatsoever, as proven by the rapid 60-foot times. Mission accomplished! (Mike Morgan)

Best of all, the Wilshire Shaker can be driven on the street without hassles. It blew minds at the famous Bob's Big Boy Friday Night Cruise in Toluca Lake, California. Yep, I drove it there on the freeway at 70 mph, a 60-mile round trip from my home base in El Monte, California. The Match Bash strategy captures much of the exciting performance of the original altered wheelbase match racers but without the race-only hassle associated with a real 9-second, fuel-burning drag car.

WILSHIRE SHAKER NOVA CONSTRUCTION OVERVIEW

A set of chained-together tennis balls keep debris out of the injector stacks during car shows. Is it true you get two dimes and a nickel out the exhaust if you drop a quarter down the stack? We don't want to find out.

Altering the wheelbase makes a dramatic difference in both the performance and visual attitude of any car. Careful considerations must be made on both points, as the modifications should be designed to improve front-to-rear weight distribution without upsetting the steering performance, and the car should look like a vintage drag racing machine.

In addition to the wheelbase changes, other visual cues complete the look on my Chevy Nova. The wheel and tire choices, hand lettering, grille-mounted tank, and injector stacks poking through the hood are all period-perfect details relating to the mid-1960s match racers the car is modeled after. The modern upgrades that make the car safe and pleasant to drive on the street are invisible.

Moving both the front and rear suspensions forward on the chassis results in much more effective weight transfer at the drag strip. With big-block power on tap, my Nova is able to launch hard and straight consistently and without drama. Careful design and execution of the modifications improved the quarter-mile performance without sacrificing street manners. (Mike Morgan)

In a scene that could have been shot in 1965, the Wilshire Shaker heats up the slicks before making a pass at the drag strip. Altered wheelbase cars like this created lifelong memories for all who saw them compete throughout the mid-1960s. While flip-top Funny Cars eclipsed them on the performance front, the bizarre appearance of the altered wheelbase quarter-milers was never to be overshadowed. Seeing such a car on the streets today leaves a similar impression. (Mike Morgan)

CHAPTER 3

RAMPAGE *DART* CONSTRUCTION OVERVIEW

Most Mopar fanatics assume the fleet of factory-altered 1965 Coronet and Belvedere B-bodies were the start of the Chrysler funny car game, but it's a fact that several altered wheelbase A-body funny cars were assembled and run by independent racers as early as September 1964. Smaller than the intermediate-size B-body, the A-body was a true compact car with a 250-pound weight advantage versus its larger sibling.

Numerous vintage magazine articles depict funnied 1964 Dodge Darts like Jack Sharkey's Chicago-based Esserman Dodge *Rampage* plus Billy Jacobs' *Kid Goat* and the Liberty Motors *Corruptor's Pup*, both out of Alabama. The thing these cars have in common is they were first campaigned with Max-Wedge power and standard 111-inch wheelbases.

Before long, each of these Darts—and plenty more, including those of Charlie Allen, Dick Landy, Bud Faubel, Gene Snow, and the Ramchargers—sprouted Race Hemis and altered wheelbases as the wild run-what-ya-brung Southern-style match race circuit heated up.

Though Jack Sharkey is deceased and Esserman Dodge is defunct, Jack's daughter, Shannon Sharkey-Millhouse, gave her blessing for our modern Match Bash tribute.

The alterations to the Dart make the most of the power being generated by its 440-cube power plant, but it's still very street-friendly. The dowdy stock look is replaced by a much more aggressive stance. This respectful clone of a vintage racer now attracts plenty of attention, and backs it up with solid performance attributes.

Plan and Prepare for Surgery

The 1965 Dart model lineup consisted of the Dart 170, Dart 270, and Dart GT. Only the 170 and 270 were available in the sedan body style with fixed B-pillars and full door frames. The upscale GT was a hardtop with no B-pillar. They're all great starting points, but the sedan's fixed B-pillar is preferred since it adds strength to the finished car and is more stable during wheelbase relocation surgery. I bought this one-owner Dart 270 sedan for $750.

One of 62,800 Dart 270s built in 1965 (including four-door models and station wagons), ours is original right down to the Music Master AM radio. Years of sitting idle in arid Southern California have taken their toll on the interior, but the body is virtually rust-free.

Since the Match Bash building style embraces a less-is-more ethos, the sagging headliner, shredded seats, and faded interior pose no problem since they'll be eliminated. The austere nature of a properly done Match Basher helps keep a lid on cost so you can devote maximum resources to the all-important engine and drivetrain.

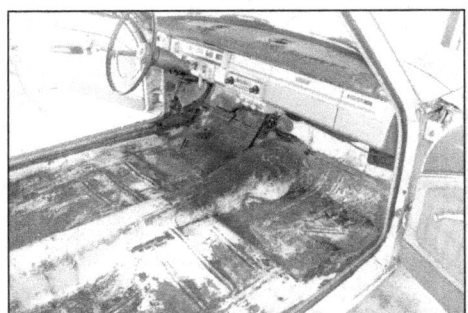

After stripping the interior, we were surprised to see so much surface rust. Fortunately, none is structural and there are no holes. This type of corrosion is typically caused by a leaky heater core that drips coolant down the firewall. It flows under the carpet and gradually attacks the surface metal. Cars with rubber floor mats are more prone to floor rust, since the non-porous rubber traps all of the moisture. Carpeting allows greater evaporation.

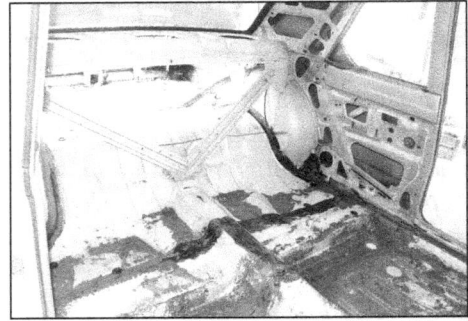

The rear floorpan and wheel houses are in better condition and exhibit much of the original Frost White paint.

After the 12-inch-forward rear axle relocation, the wheel houses invade the space shown here. The entire inner body structure and window regulators must be sliced away to make room.

CHAPTER 3

The rear side-window regulators are removed. Think twice about trashing these items. Since window regulators often wear out over time, chances are you can sell serviceable take-offs to another Dart owner in need. Our spare bits were donated to a Mopar collector. We chose to keep the glass, since it will be retained and located in the permanently raised position by fabricated supports.

Move the Rear Wheels

With the car supported on a level concrete surface, the stock rear axle centerline is established by using a weighted string. The stock Dart wheelbase is 111 inches. By moving the string forward in small increments, you can visualize the final appearance after surgery by positioning a dummy tire in line with the hanging string.

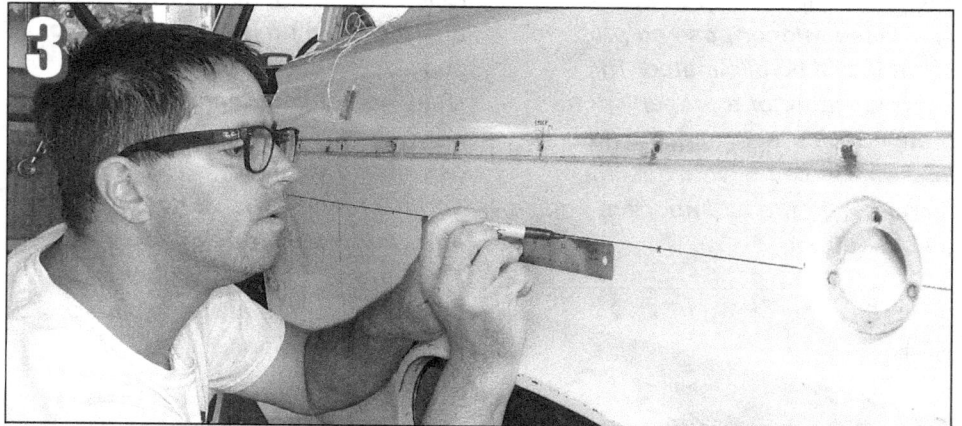

Once the axle relocation distance is decided, a long bubble level and felt-tip marker are used as a guide to apply the vertical and horizontal cut lines to both sides of the body. Try to position all cuts along flat sections of sheetmetal to minimize bodywork complexity. Use symmetrical reference points—such as the body trim fastener holes—to ensure the cut lines are identical on both sides of the body.

We could move the axle as much as 20 inches, as Jack Sharkey did, but the result exaggerates the rear overhang and borders on the grotesque—in a good way. Conversely, a 6-inch move is too subtle and understated. These cars need to be brash, but too much is too much. We settled on a 12-inch move as the best balance between aesthetic appeal and function. Remember, the more the rear axle moves forward, the greater the impact on static and dynamic weight distribution. Going too far can yield a self-destructive wheelie machine.

The external cut lines have been established and applied to both sides of the body with a marker. At all times, the body must be firmly supported in numerous places to prevent it from sagging during surgery. The best strategy is to separate the suspension module from the car and roll it forward under the shell in one piece. Cutting the suspension module into sub-assemblies adds tremendous complication and invites chassis misalignment hassles. Mini-tubbing and other suspension modifications will be performed after the wheelbase has been altered. The 12-inch panel marked with "X" will be eliminated.

On most cars, the window sill is an ideal horizontal reference point to confirm the car is sitting at a perfectly horizontal orientation. Thin wooden shims made from paint-mixing sticks can be placed between the jack stand supports and the vehicle frame to fine-tune the support network and center the bubble level reading.

Seven jack stands are used to support the car. You'll be moving around inside the car during surgery, so make sure each jack stand is secure with no gaps to allow settling or other vehicle movement.

Do not support the body by the rear axle or springs, as they must be free to move once the suspension module has been cut free from the chassis. Instead, support the body so the rear springs hang free with only a slight load on the tires. If you can't turn them by hand with a slight drag on the floor, shim the body on the jack stands until you can, but always keep the car level. You don't want to compress the leaf springs with any load or they'll push the floor up after the final separation cut is made. This will cause major alignment headaches.

The back of the body is supported by jack stands placed beneath the quarter panels and in the center of the rear bumper.

Rampage Dart Road Test

The best thing about this car is the fact that it's semi-finished. Sure it runs and drives like a freshly built hot rod—because it is. But the raw bodywork, faded paint, and general butch attitude sets us free from the worry associated with driving a show poodle. We always say, "Either you own your car, or your car owns you." There is no doubt, we *own* this one! Dust, road rash, and paint chips are of absolutely no consequence and we love it.

One surprising detail is how the pseudo Max-Wedge loves to idle in slow traffic and starts up with a wild roar. Sure, you have to pump the gas eight times before twisting the key, but once it lights it's as docile as an Imperial. There is no hesitation and throttle tip-in is smooth with no lean bogs or other drivability hassles. Frankly, my previous experience with a Max-Wedge-equipped 1964 Dodge Polara taught me to fear the cross ram. That old Polara used to backfire, stall, and surge.

Not so the A&A cross ram. Though the twin 500-cfm Edelbrocks yield a thirsty 11 mpg, none of the Polara's evil traits are present. And get this: The carburetors are box stock with none of the confusing cross-jetting that's supposed to be part of the Max-Wedge experience. On the open road the car cruises along at 3,000 rpm but jumps ahead when the gas pedal is floored. No, there aren't any wheelies (it'd probably take another 100 hp to make that happen) but the altered wheelbase really does work. Case in point: Even though there's a 3.23:1-geared open differential in the rear axle for now, it's nearly impossible to make the hard M/T slicks spin! You can power brake for big smoke shows, but the 48/52 front/rear static-weight distribution grows to something close to 20/80 at full throttle (0/100 equals a wheelie). The nose lifts a few inches away from the leaf springs, the rear axle pinion snubber rises to contact the floor, and the car moves out with no tire spin at all. If this were a standard wheelbase Dart with 440 power and those hard slicks, it'd be a useless smoke machine.

Another benefit of the altered wheelbase is the crisp handling that comes from the wheelbase reduction. This is especially noticed during low-speed parking maneuvers. The thing feels almost like a circus clown car when you crank the steering to full lock and drive in tiny circles. Yes, I'll surely pull it all apart some day in the not-too-distant future and ruin everything by making it nice and shiny. Until then, let's drive!

Here, you can see the orientation of the trio of jack stands.

Jack stands also support the middle of the body. Place them directly beneath the rocker sills as close to the outside of the car as possible. They must not contact the floorpan, since it will be moved forward during the operation.

The front of the car must be supported at the frame, not the lower control arms or any other part of the front suspension. The body shell must be prevented from doing any type of bouncing as you move around inside the car during work.

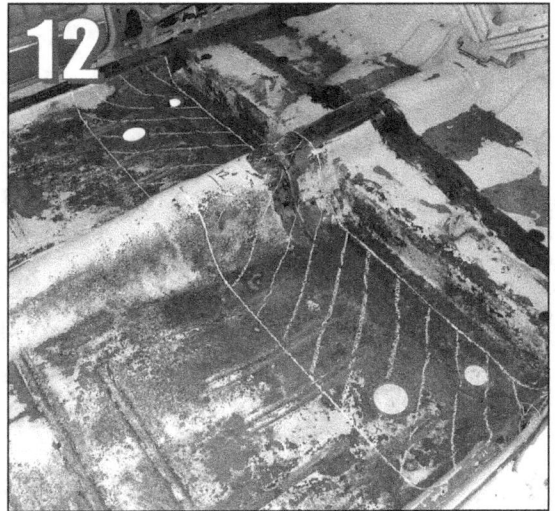

Inside the car, a 12-inch section of the floorpan (where back-seat passengers used to put their feet) is marked for removal. Once docked, the relocated suspension module will close the resulting gap. Even though this Dart spent its life in California, the floor has minor surface rust. Fortunately, there are no holes to be patched. Always start with the cleanest car you can find to avoid rust-repair hassles.

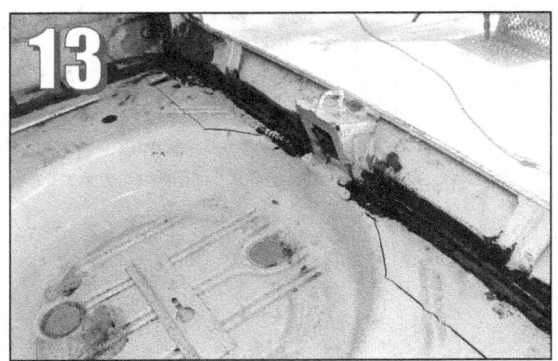

At the rear of the trunk, the highlighter-drawn cut line shows where the trunk floor will be sliced from the body shell. There are rectangular frame extensions beneath the trunk floor that must also be cut.

Inside the trunk, the highlighter-drawn cut line indicates the perimeter of the body and trunk floor section that will be trimmed from the body shell and rolled forward as part of the one-piece suspension module. Several 1/8-inch holes are drilled at the intersections of the cut lines. They are drilled from the outside of the car. By connecting the holes with a felt-tip marker, we see what the cut looks like from inside. Identical markings are applied on the other side of the trunk. We cut horizontally through the gas fill tube opening because moving the cut above or below it would be into body creases that would be difficult to recreate and smooth during finish bodywork.

Dale Snoke makes the first incision using a combination of tools to cut the metal. A pneumatic cut-off wheel and electric reciprocating saw make quick, clean cuts while a plasma cutter is used where access is limited. Be sure all flammable material has been removed from the work area.

To get access, the boxed sections of the rocker sills must be attacked from the inside, bottom, and outside. Make all cuts as straight and clean as possible to ease the rejoining process. As fast as it is, the plasma cutter leaves a layer of slag on cut lines that must be ground away prior to welding. The cut-off wheel and reciprocating saw are preferred because they make cleaner cuts.

CHAPTER 3

Here's the 12-inch floor section after removal. It goes without saying there will be no room for a back seat after the rear suspension module has been moved forward 12 inches.

With its entire perimeter cut free from the body shell, the suspension module is ready to roll…literally. With a helper to make sure it moves freely without snagging or getting crooked, the module easily rolls forward 12 inches until it docks with the body.

Jockey the suspension module carefully until the body lines are perfectly aligned and the wheelbase measurement is equal from side to side. The process of rejoining everything starts with the skin of the car because alignment problems are most obvious here. A series of low-heat spot welds rejoins the quarter panels. A continuous bead of weld will come later after the rest of the module has been welded firm.

On the driver's side, the stock gas filler has been severed but we'll patch it back together since we're keeping the Dart's stock 16-gallon gas tank. Thanks to the multitude of jack stands supporting the body, note how the body lines line right up after the suspension module has been docked with the body shell.

HOW TO BUILD ALTERED WHEELBASE CARS

With spot welds securing the quarter-panel skins, we go inside where the docked suspension module is welded into its new location, 12 inches ahead of where the factory put it. Flat steel-welded patches close the occasional gap. Never booger-weld wide gaps because strength is compromised.

Here's the stock interior before we got started. Notice the long distance between the door post and the wheel tub. With the 12-inch move, the wheelbase shrinks from 111 to 99 inches. But, since we'll move the front axle centerline ahead 4 inches, the final wheelbase will be 103 inches.

Rolling the suspension module forward leaves a 12-inch gap in the trunk that's easily filled with welded sheet steel. The rear frame extensions are reconnected with heavy-wall 1½ x 3-inch square tubing.

The gaps in the quarter panels are filled with hand-formed sheet steel. Rather than attempt to recreate the sharp horizontal body crease, Dale uses two patches with a joint running along the crease. A series of low-heat spot welds minimizes panel distortion.

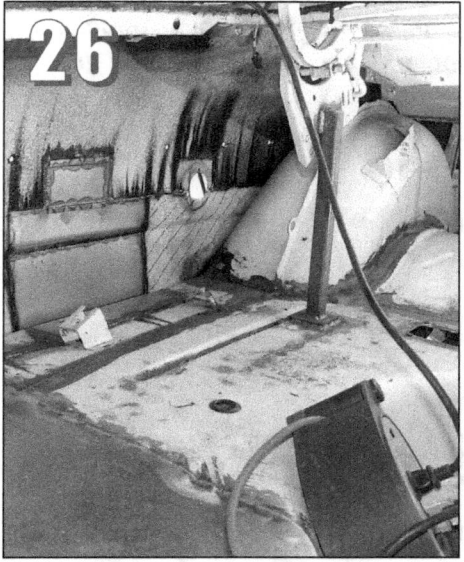

We're keeping the stock 16-gallon gas tank on this street and strip mauler, so rather than patch the fuel fill hole, Dale rejoined the severed halves so the stock filler tube can be retained. The patchwork can be seen here. Also note the trunk floor patch and simple, square-tube support linking the trunk lid hinge mount to the trunk floor. Previously, the hinge mounts were joined to the wheel houses before relocation.

The bottom edge of the quarter-panel patch is rolled under to match the existing profile. After final bodywork, the surgery scars will be invisible.

CHAPTER 3

The passenger side is handled the same way. By moving the rear suspension module as a one-piece unit, the wheelbase alteration process is greatly simplified. Though structural integrity has been restored at this point, Dale leaves the car on the jack stands for better access to the underside for final welding.

The diagonal, speaker shelf support braces contribute to torsional rigidity, and are welded back in place after trimming.

A heavy coat of Rust-Oleum keeps the bare steel from flash rusting until the car goes in for its body and paint makeover. The trunk area will eventually be covered in Zolotone spatter paint.

The passenger-side patchwork is complete. Since this Dart is a 270 model, it has more chrome gingerbread than the base Dart 170 model. The 270-specific horizontal body moldings have been removed but the mounting holes (19 per side) must be welded shut. Smooth flanks—devoid of chrome trim—allow greater freedom to choose an attractive paint and graphics treatment.

We could have stopped here and still turned plenty of heads. But the full Match Bash treatment is only achieved when the front wheels are altered as well. We'll get to that soon.

In hindsight, the stock rear-axle placement looks almost awkward. The altered wheelbase treatment gives any car a certain dynamic energy, as if the chassis is eager to blast out from under the body, even standing still.

Install Subframe Connectors

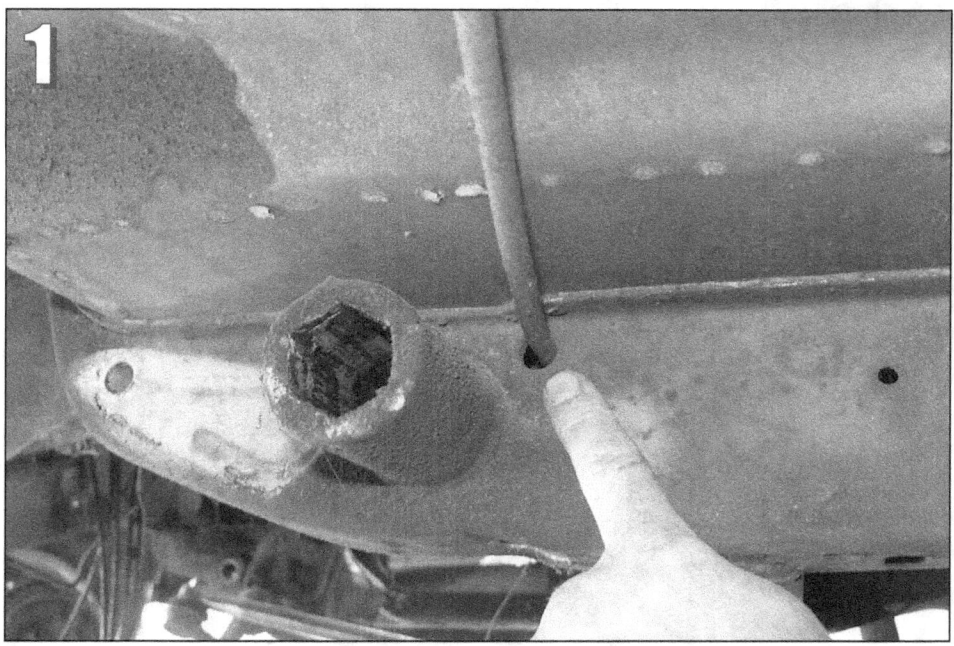

1 With the rear axle relocation work completed, it's time to add subframe connectors for improved strength. As the name implies, we're connecting the front and rear vehicle subframes with welded lengths of 2 x 3-inch square steel tubing. The forward ends of the tubes contact the back of the torsion bar crossmember. The steel fuel line must be re-routed from the stock position to eliminate interference.

2 Use a long straightedge and pen to mark the underside of the floorpan with a 2-inch-wide path from the rear subframes straight ahead to the torsion bar crossmember. Since only a portion of the floorpan drops down and interferes with the planned tubes, only remove the metal that is in the way, as shown. A reciprocating saw makes the cleanest, straightest cuts.

3 As seen from beneath the car, only remove the metal that obstructs the square tubes from fitting up against the floor. Note the perfect 90-degree corner cuts that reduce the need for patching.

4 Since the Dart's rear frame has been moved forward 12 inches, the distance between the torsion bar crossmember and rear subframes is less than stock. We started with a 34-inch length of 2 x 3-inch square tubing. This allows a bit of extra length to contour the rearward end for a close fit to the shape of the rear subframe for a clean merge. A paper pattern transfers the subframe shape to the end of the tube to aid the trimming process.

With the tubing connectors trimmed for a close fit between the forward torsion bar crossmember and rear subframe, each one is pushed up against the floor and through the clearance slices. Then, Dale welds each end in place. Here he welds the rear of the passenger-side subframe connector.

For maximum strength, a continuous bead of weld is applied between the floor skin and the new connectors. Because the initial floor cuts were very accurate, the weld fills all gaps and there is no need for rubber or silicone seam sealer. This is the driver-side subframe connector as viewed from inside the car.

Here's the completed installation on the passenger side.

With the beefy steel subframe connectors fully welded in position, the Dart's unibody is ready for the stress and strain of drag racing. Further fortification will come from the 6-point roll bar we'll install.

Relocate Rear Leaf Springs

Though most Mopars are capable of swallowing up pretty big rear meats, our choice of Radir 15 x 10-inch square-tread retro slicks and 15 x 7-inch American Racing Torq-Thrust D wheels (3⅝-inch back spacing) takes up much more space than the stock 13-inch factory rubber.

Here's the stock rear-leaf-spring position with the slicks in place. Notice how the sidewalls rub against the springs. Though wheel spacers are sometimes a valid solution, they can shift the problem outboard and cause fender lip contact on the other side of the tire. Plus, they can fail under high-traction conditions.

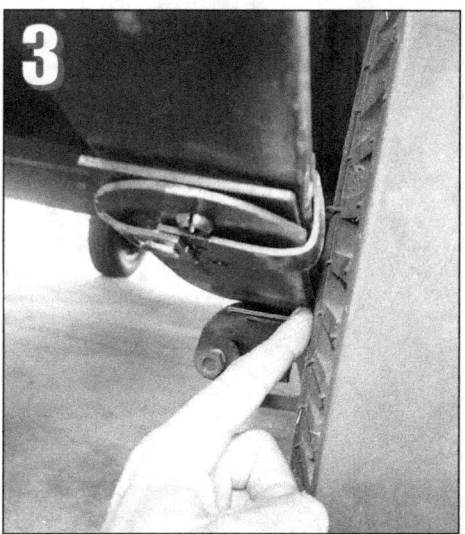

A closer view proves we need to relocate the leaf springs inboard, beneath the frame rails, to regain adequate sidewall clearance.

After supporting the body on jack stands, the entire rear suspension must be removed for frame access. At this point, the stock 7¼-inch rear axle is still being used for mock-up purposes. It'll be replaced by a stronger 8¾-inch axle soon.

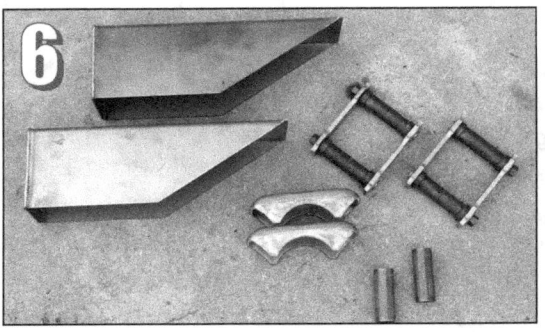

Here's a final look at the Dart's stock frame rails.

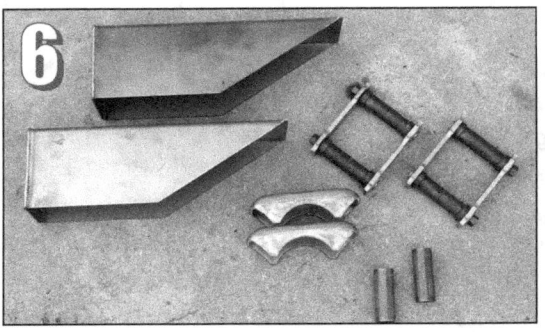

The Mopar Performance leaf spring re-location kit (PN P4876558AB) sells for around $160 and includes everything you see here plus a detailed instruction sheet.

CHAPTER 3

After cleaning the work area with a wire wheel and grinder, a reciprocating saw is used to remove a wedge-shape slice from the bottom of the frame on each side of the chassis. Make sure the cuts are straight, horizontal, and symmetrical from one side of the chassis to the other. Torching or plasma-cutting the frame is not recommended, as it leaves rough edges, which can introduce error.

We're retaining the cable-actuated emergency brakes so the cable brackets must be carefully removed from each side of the frame. We drilled out the spot welds instead of chiseling the brackets to prevent damage and torn metal.

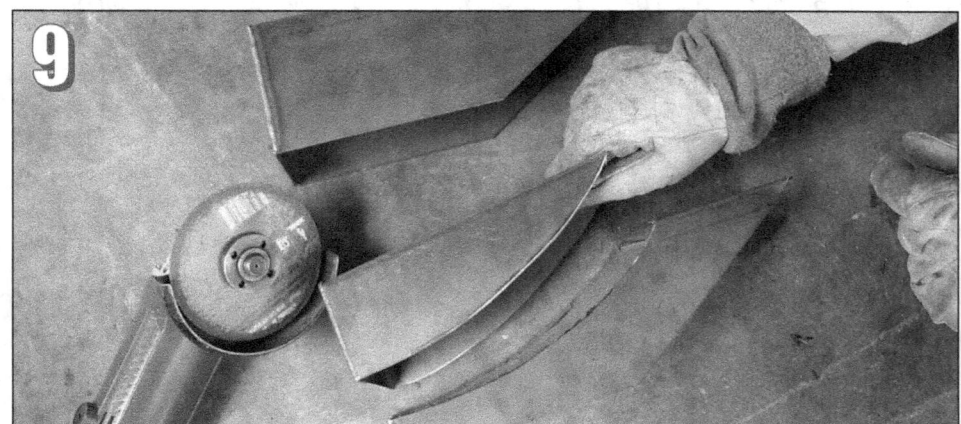

The MP frame insert sections (top) are extra large to allow for changes in the location of the forward leaf spring eye. We've only removed a small section of the stock frame so we trimmed the insert (center) to suit our needs with a cut-off wheel. The part was then used as a template to trim the other side.

While it is possible to manipulate axle thrust angle, pinion angle, ride height, and total wheelbase by repositioning the forward spring eye's through-bolt location, we stuck with the Dart's stock specifications. A felt-tip marker transfers the through-bolt location onto the new frame insert. Using the stock spring hangars as a marking guide ensures perfect accuracy and side-to-side symmetry. The holes are drilled on the work bench for convenience prior to welding the frame inserts in place.

After confirming proper horizontal and lateral orientation, Dale applies a continuous bead of weld to the perimeter of each frame section insert.

The emergency-brake cable brackets are welded back to their original positions once the inserts are in place.

HOW TO BUILD ALTERED WHEELBASE CARS

RAMPAGE DART CONSTRUCTION OVERVIEW

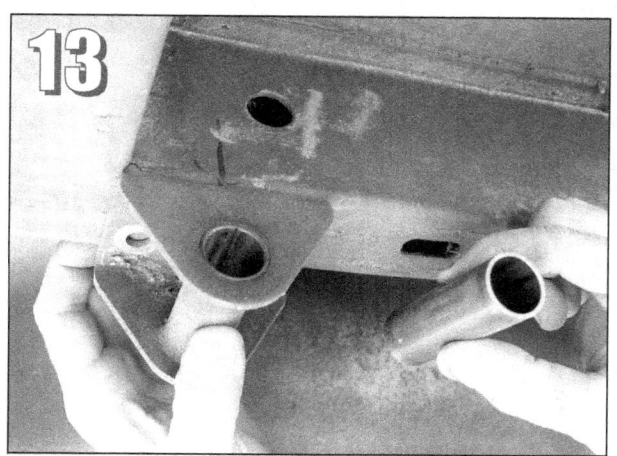

The MP kit includes two pieces of tubing (right) to accept the upper shackle bushings at the rear of the springs. They can be inserted into holes drilled into the rear frame rails or welded to the bottoms of the frame rails with gussets. Dale went one better and simply reused the stock Dart brackets (left).

With the leaf springs bolted in place, their new inboard location beneath the frame rails can be seen. This is the passenger side of the axle, looking forward. Notice that the stock axle spring pads sit well outboard of the new pads included with the kit. We'll establish a 5-degree nose-down pinion angle and weld these new pads to the 8¾-inch rear axle when it is ready for installation later. The MP spring relocation kit reduces the distance between the leaf springs by 7 inches, split evenly from side to side.

By welding the Dart shackle brackets to the bottoms of the frame rails, the vehicle ride height is increases by 3½ inches without resorting to added shackle length. Extra ride height is desirable for proper Match Bash stance. The boxed bulkhead to the left is where the shackle brackets were previously located in the stock configuration.

Where there was full interference contact, we now have 3½ inches of sidewall clearance on each end of the axle. The minimum safe distance is 1 inch. Remember, as the car takes corners, the tire carcass shifts and can rub the springs without adequate clearance.

Compare this photo with the one showing the stock leaf spring layout and you'll see a big difference. The entire job took one day.

HOW TO BUILD ALTERED WHEELBASE CARS

CHAPTER 3

Install Mini-Tubs

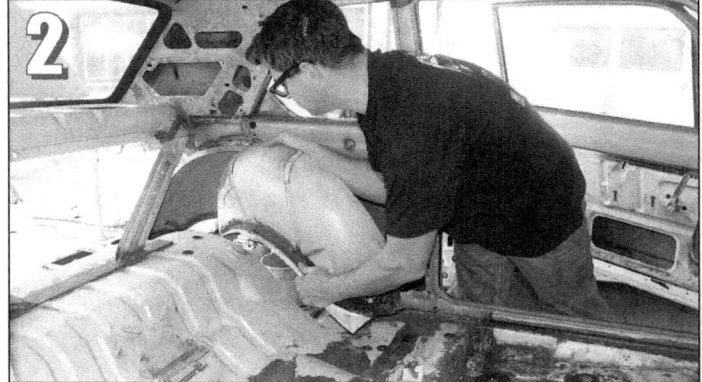

1. The mini-tub process eliminates the wasted space shown here and delivers an extra 2 inches of tire clearance on each side of the car. The pinch-welded flange is where Dodge originally joined the wheel tub to the floorpan of the Dart. Many Match Bash candidates exhibit similar architecture in this area. If your tires exhibit mystery slices on the inner part of the tread surface, contact here is the likely cause.

2. A reciprocating saw and cut-off wheel are used to slice the stock wheel tubs down the middle and around their bases where they attach to the floorpan.

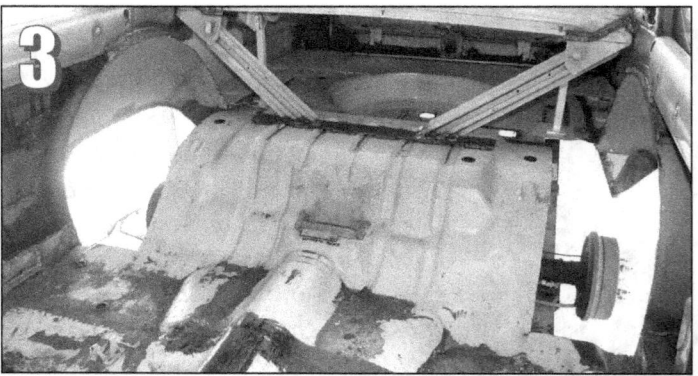

3. Here's what you want to see after the stock tubs have been sliced away from their stock resting places. All cuts must be as straight and clean as possible for a sanitary outcome.

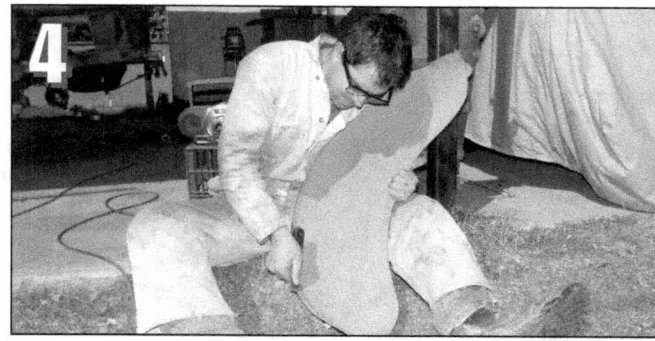

4. Even on non-undercoated California cars like this Dart, you'll find heavily sprayed-on sound deadener in the wheel tubs. It must be scraped away at the adjoining edges where welding will take place.

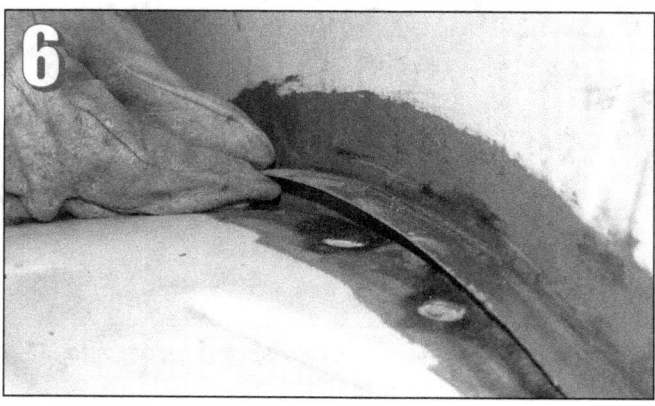

6. Here, the flanged edges of the tubs are set down on top of the floorpan. With all sound deadener and undercoating scraped away, the two panels can be welded together.

5. The 2 inches of additional tub are gained by simply remounting the wheel tub sections on top of the existing floorpan cut line. Daylight shines through the gaps that result when the tubs are pulled inboard. On this altered wheelbase Dart, the space usually occupied by the rear side window regulators has been gutted to make room for the 12-inch forward relocation of the rear axle and floor module.

RAMPAGE DART CONSTRUCTION OVERVIEW

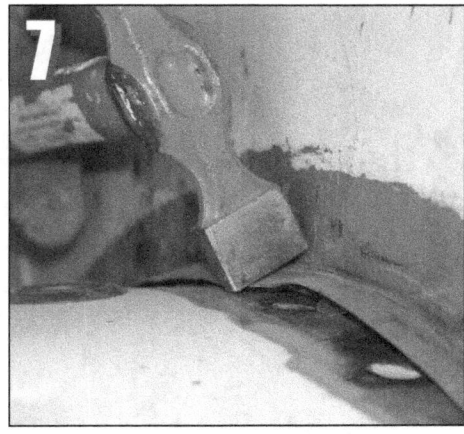

Some areas of the tubs must be flattened to match the contours of the floorpan using a body hammer. Reducing the gaps allows better welds when they are joined together.

After making sure the tubs are correctly aligned with the floorpan, a continuous bead of weld is applied.

Here's a look at the fully welded tub on the passenger side of the car. Notice how the 90-degree corners merge easily with the floorpan. Making the filler strips is next.

Dale uses a cut-off wheel to trim a pair of 2-inch-wide strips from a sheet of .030-inch-thick steel.

The 2-inch wheel tub gaps are patched with the welded-in filler strips. Dale went over the top with seamless welds to ensure water tightness and to prevent tire smoke from entering the cabin during burnouts.

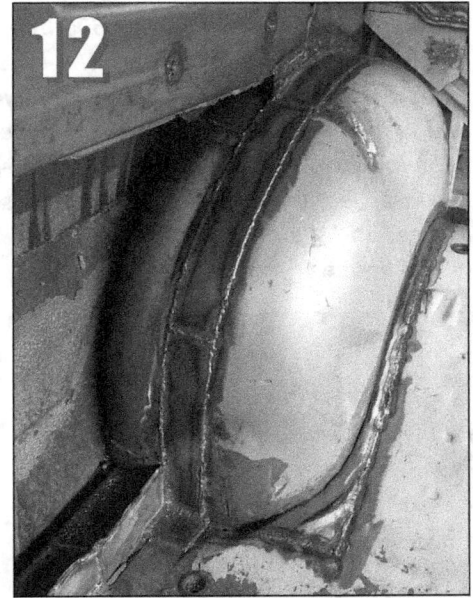

After all the welding is completed, the widened wheel tub looks right at home. We're not concerned with maintaining strict factory appearances on this altered wheelbase match-race tribute car, so we won't bother with grinding the welds or smoothing the work with filler. In true funny car fashion, a liberal coat of Zolotone trunk paint will be applied later.

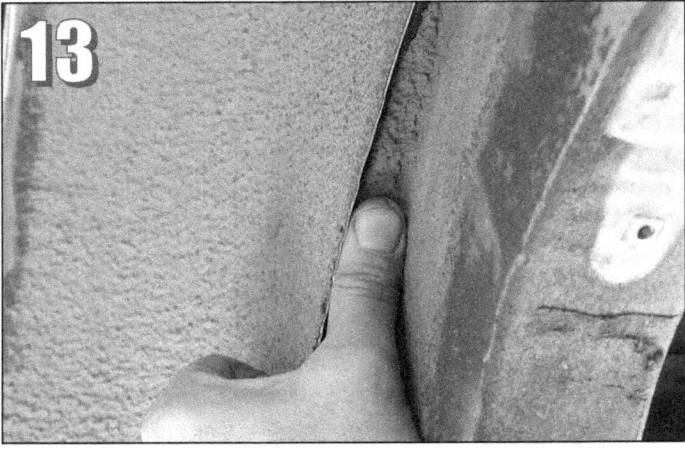

After mini-tubbing, you can barely get a finger between the wheel tubs and frame rails. Tire sidewall clearance has increased by 2 inches so there's no chance of contact with the Dart's Radir 15 x 10-inch nostalgia drag slicks.

HOW TO BUILD ALTERED WHEELBASE CARS

CHAPTER 3

Upgrade and Narrow Rear Axle

The stock 7¼-inch rear axle (foreground) measures 57½ inches drum-to-drum. It was originally designed for Slant Six applications and will quickly fail behind a big-block V-8. By contrast, the Chrysler 8¾-inch axle is rugged enough to handle as much as 600 hp. Ours came from a junked 1968 Dodge A100 van. The bare housing measures a whopping 56½ inches—not including brakes and axles. We need to narrow it 6 inches to arrive at a 50½-inch width. Once the axle shafts and drum brakes are installed, the drum-to-drum dimension will be 55½-inches, and the big slicks will easily fit inside the Dart's wheel houses.

A side benefit of the axle upgrade is the 10 x 2½-inch brakes that'll replace the Dart's original 9 x 1¾-inch drums (foreground) for extra stopping power.

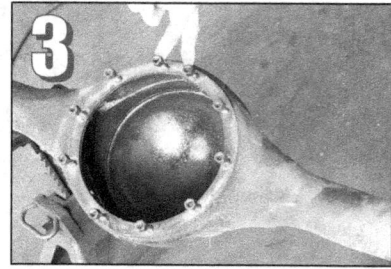

My fingers point out the two close-spaced studs that denote the top of the Mopar 8¾-inch axle housing. Make sure you have the housing right side up during the modification process or the welded-on axle ends and spring pads will be upside down.

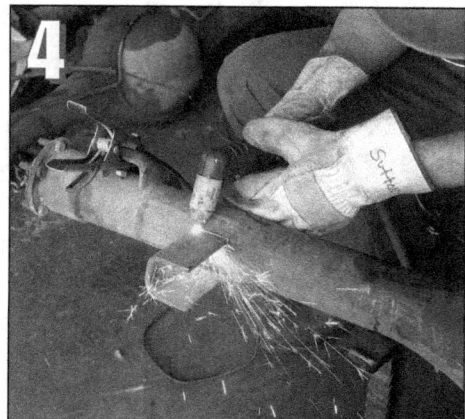

Mando Sutton uses a plasma cutter to remove the A100 van's useless shock-absorber mounting brackets and spring perches. They'll obstruct the cutting and welding operations and aren't compatible with the Dart's leaf spring position.

The goal is to reduce the total housing width from 56½ to 50½ inches. Since the welded-on outer axle bearing carriers will be reused, we must remember not to simply measure 3 inches from the outmost ends and chop. Instead, the correct way is to measure in 3 inches from where the axle bearing carriers meet the axle housing tubes, and make the cuts there. Cuts must be made on the inside edge of the cut lines to compensate for the 1/8-inch thickness of the chop saw blade. As they say, measure twice; cut once.

HOW TO BUILD ALTERED WHEELBASE CARS

RAMPAGE DART CONSTRUCTION OVERVIEW

The severed housing ends are mounted in the lathe and the welds securing the outer axle bearing carrier ends are removed.

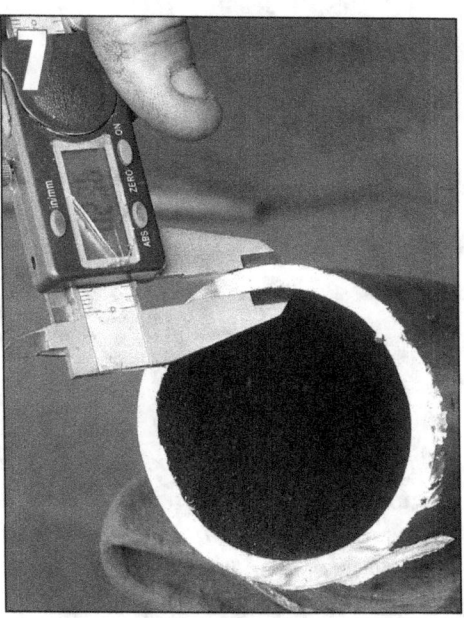

The stock 8¾-inch axle housing is fabricated from several sections of welded steel stampings and features rugged 1/4-inch-thick axle tubes. Though they are swaged into thinner sections where the differential bolts up, Mando says the stock housing is good for 10.99-second ETs before it starts to bend.

To guarantee perfect alignment of the outer axle bearing carriers during re-installation, the Suttons use an empty differential fitted with precision hubs in place of the carrier bearings. The steel alignment bar floats in the hubs and will ensure accurate installation.

The cleaned and chamfered outer axle bearing carrier is ready to be reunited with the narrowed axle housing. The chamfered end yields excellent weld penetration. Note how the alignment bar fits through the steel cap bolted to the carrier studs.

With the ends aligned in the fixture, they are MIG welded to the axle tubes. After surgery, the total width of the bare housing is exactly 50½ inches.

Always install new axle seals after surgery since the originals are destroyed by heat during the welding process. If you don't have a proper seal-driving tool, a steel tube or socket wrench with 1.7-inch O.D. will do the trick.

HOW TO BUILD ALTERED WHEELBASE CARS

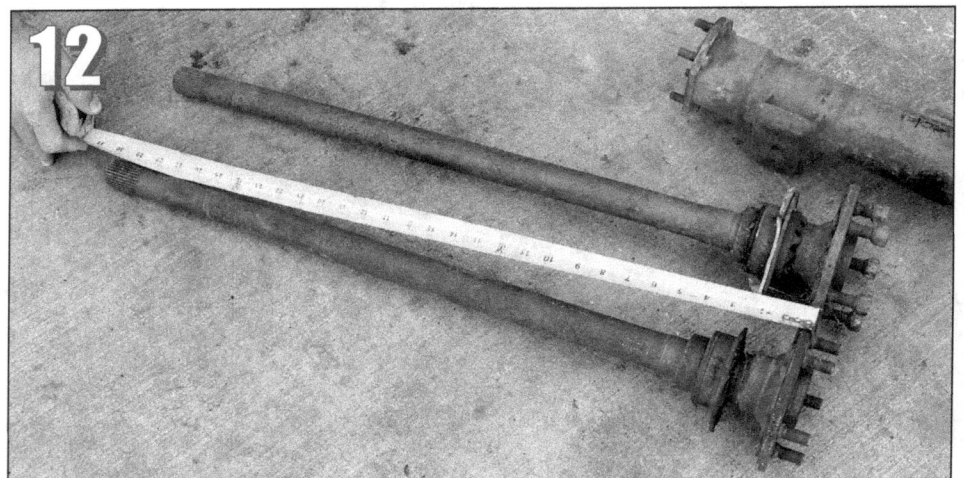

Unlike many other rear axle types, Mopar 8¾-inch axle shafts are the same length from side-to-side. These Dodge A100 van axle shafts measure 30 inches. Like the axle housing, we need to remove 3 inches from each shaft, then cut in new splines.

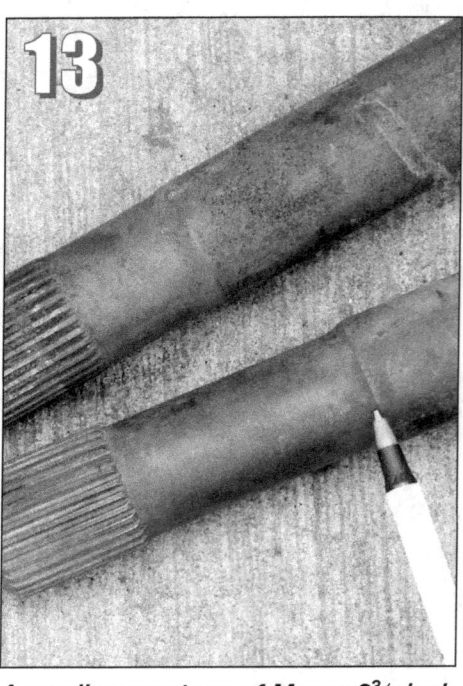

After careful measurement, the chop saw removes 3 inches from the end of each axle. Make sure they're resting flat on the saw table so you get straight cuts.

A small percentage of Mopar 8¾-inch axle shafts (as well as some Fords) feature extra-long 4-inch undercuts (shown at the pen tip). Unless you are building a super-narrow, rail-dragster-style axle, there isn't enough material diameter at the ends to allow re-splining. Our A100 axles (top) have 3-inch undercuts; no problem with our needed 3-inch chop job.

Next, the axles are chucked up in Sutton's Goodway lathe. In three steps, we removed .038 inch to achieve a constant diameter for successful re-splining.

Here, the pen points to the gradual radius put into the transition from the freshly machined and non-machined axle surfaces. This eliminates the stress riser and potential failure point a sheer 90-degree merge would create.

RAMPAGE DART CONSTRUCTION OVERVIEW

The vertical mill cuts one .040-inch-deep spline at a time using a specially designed cutting tool that spins at high RPM. A dividing head on the mill precisely controls the length and depth of each cut and—in this case—delivers the stock Chrysler 30-spline axle end specification.

The pen tip points at the .187-inch-deep factory surface hardening that is only mildly affected by the .040-inch-deep spline cuts (right). The Suttons say re-splined stock axle shafts are safe for 3,400-pound cars running 11.0 seconds with an automatic or 12.0 seconds with more brutal stick shifts. At about $140 per pair, re-splining makes pretty good economic sense.

The shortened and re-splined axle shafts are test fit inside the 8¾-inch differential to confirm proper side-gear engagement. Then, the differential is installed in the narrowed housing and the axle shafts are installed with grease on the splines. Removal will leave a witness mark on the splines showing the depth of engagement. You want to see at least 1 inch of engagement for full-torque capacity.

After we install a set of extra-length drag shocks (PN 4529515) and an adjustable pinion snubber (PN P3690182) from Mopar Performance, the Dart's upgraded rear suspension will be ready for anything the Max-Wedge can dish out. For the time being, an open differential with mild 3.23:1 gearing is in place, but we'll upgrade soon to a 3.91:1 Sure Grip for maximum traction.

After axle width reduction, there's plenty of clearance between the leaf springs and fender lips.

HOW TO BUILD ALTERED WHEELBASE CARS

CHAPTER 3

Install Roll Bar

It's a fact that you've got to install a roll bar if your car's running fast and you want to take it to a sanctioned strip. You need to add a 6-point roll bar as soon as you break the 11.99-second threshold in the quarter-mile (or 7.49 seconds in the 1/8-mile). We're expecting to run mid-11s, so it's time to act. There are no commonly available roll bar kits on the market for the 1963 Dart, but after measuring the interior height (42½ inches), inside width at the sills (57¼ inches), belt line (53 inches), and roof supports (46½ inches), it became clear that the Competition Engineering C3123A 1967–1976 Mopar A-body roll bar hoop would fit. Bent from 1¾-inch-long, .134-inch-thick mild steel, Competition Engineering roll bar kits are sold as an application-specific main hoop that's supported by a universal-fit strut kit. In this case, the 8-point universal-fit strut kit carries PN C3000.

The NHRA rulebook states in the General Regulations section: "All roll bars must be within 6 inches of the rear, or side, of the driver's head, extended in height at least 3 inches above the driver's helmet with driver in normal driving position." As delivered, the main hoop is 1 inch too tall to fit inside the Dart, so Funny Car Farm honcho "Jungle Dale" Snoke uses a tape measure to mark it for trimming. In this gutted Match Bash car there will be no fabric headliner, so the vertical legs of the hoop are cut to provide 1 inch of clearance to the roof skin. This puts it well within the mandated 6-inch-maximum distance from the driver's helmet.

Trimming the main hoop height is best done in a series of small cuts to avoid going too far. A chop saw is best, though you can get by with a hack saw if you're careful to make clean, even cuts.

On unit-construction cars (that means virtually every popular Mopar) the NHRA mandates that each tube and strut must be welded to a 6 x 6-inch, 1/8-inch-minimum-thickness steel plate that's welded to the floorpan (it is also permissible to bolt these plates to the floor with a minimum of four 3/8-inch bolts as long as a second plate is also present beneath to "sandwich" the floorpan). The Competition Engineering kit comes complete with six mounting plates. Keep in mind that while these plates can be formed to fit the underlying floor surface, they cannot be trimmed in a fashion that reduces their original 6 x 6-inch size. Here, Dale taps the main hoop-mounting plate to center it prior to welding.

The NHRA rule book also states that the rear struts must be welded to the main hoop at an angle that is at least 30 degrees from vertical. While it is legal to mount them as far as 5 inches down from the top of the main hoop, the most practical approach is to mount them to the horizontal span of the hoop as shown here. Using a magnetic protractor, Dale establishes a legal-eagle 50-degree angle that places the feet of the struts conveniently against a section of floor that's backed by the Dart's subframe, which ties the car together nicely.

RAMPAGE DART CONSTRUCTION OVERVIEW

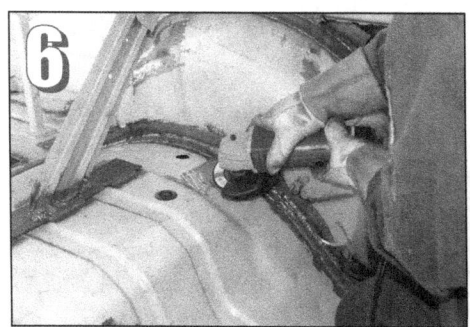

All paint, body seam sealer, and surface rust scale must be ground away prior to welding the mounting plates.

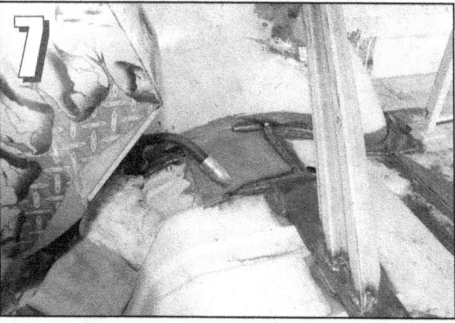

To get the plates to conform to the Dart's irregular floorpan surfaces, Dale welds a small section in place, and then hammers it flat with the floor. He then welds the gaps before using the hammer again to form the next section. This method is a foolproof alternative to attempts at forming the plates on the work bench with a hammer and vise.

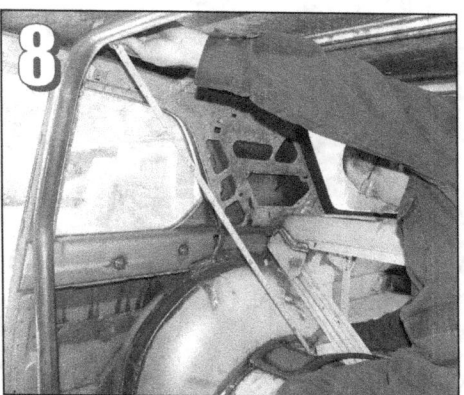

A final distance measurement is taken before the rear struts are cut for the final time. We need them to be $40\frac{1}{2}$ inches, but Dale leaves an extra inch to accommodate the 50-degree cut he'll put at the foot so it merges with the mounting plates without creating gaps.

Creeping up on the orientation of the foot allows a clean merge with the mounting plate. The small pile of remnants is made one by one as the ideal shape is sought. After each cut, the strut is test fitted and marked where further trimming is needed.

Once the strut is trimmed to its ideal configuration, it is tested on the opposite side of the hoop. Thanks to Dale's continuous effort to maintain symmetry, the strut is an exact fit on either side of the hoop. Rather than go through the hand-fitting process all over again, he simply transfers the cut line onto the other strut—in one chop, it's ready for installation on the opposite end of the hoop.

The door struts must be mounted so they intersect the occupant's elbow and shoulder (as shown) to be NHRA compliant.

HOW TO BUILD ALTERED WHEELBASE CARS

CHAPTER 3

With the upper mounting point marked on the hoop, the door strut is cut to 26 inches and the floor mounting-plate location can be established. Heavy cardboard protects window glass from grinding and welding damage. Unprotected glass will pick up hot grit and leave permanent craters you'll never polish out.

As with all other mounting plates, the grinder removes all paint and surface rust from the area to be welded.

Again, Dale uses the hammer-and-tack technique to get the 6 x 6-inch mounting plates to sit flush with the contours of the floor.

Here's a look at the finished mounting plate after it's been hammered and welded down.

The final step is the installation of the horizontal cross brace. The one supplied in the universal-fit Competition Engineering strut kit is 56 1/2 inches, some 7 inches too long for this application. We'll trim it to fit.

While one end of the cross brace is already notched to fit the main hoop, the other end must be notched after cutting. This can be done with a simple grinder and some patience but Dale prefers to use this inexpensive tube notcher from Central Machinery. You can find these at Harbor Freight for well under $50. Just clamp it in a vise and, using a 1 3/4-inch hole saw mounted in a drill motor, it makes short work of the notching process.

HOW TO BUILD ALTERED WHEELBASE CARS

18 Here's the completed notch. The tubing notcher can cut angles from 0 to 45 degrees in 1-degree increments. Get one, it's ten times faster and cleaner than freehand notching with a grinder.

19 Knowing that the rule book says the cross brace must be positioned "no more than 4 inches below, and not above, the driver's shoulders" the bubble level helps ensure horizontal orientation. But remember, if the car isn't sitting level, the bubble reading will throw you off. The safe method is to measure up from the floor to ensure horizontal cross-brace installation.

20 Here's a look at the completed job. We'll add seat belt tabs to the cross brace and padding later. While the Competition Engineering kit also includes optional hoop supports that run diagonally from the hoop to the driveshaft tunnel on each side (and boost the roll bar to eight-point status), we'll skip them for now as they are not required for the mid-11-second ETs this car will be running.

21 Unless you're dealing with chrome moly, all tubes in a mild steel kit like this must be painted to prevent rust. We're crazy about Rust-Oleum oil-based enamel brush paint. If you lay it on super heavy and let it dry for a few weeks, it wet sands out to a mirror finish that's much tougher than anything coming from a rattle can. Plus, there's no overspray hassle so masking isn't required. We call it the poor man's powder coat. Make ours Gloss Black or Smoke Gray.

22 With the roll bar installed, we're ready to install a potent Max-Wedge and hit the match race circuit where we'll soon face the Rat-powered Wilshire Shaker Nova.

23 Seeking the ultimate in weight reduction, many match racers—the original Rampage Dart included—turned to lightweight fiberglass bucket seats as the competition heated up. Though there are plenty of modern racing bucket seats available, most are too modern looking for our retro tastes. Appletree Automotive offers these low-back seat shells (PN 7250) that are a perfect match for the seats used in many vintage match racers. Dale Snoke whipped up the rugged mounting brackets.

CHAPTER 3

Install Straight Front Axle

1 The front fenders, bumper, and valance are removed to provide working access, but we left the hood bolted in place. That's because we used a weighted string to mark the stock axle centerline on the hood skin with a marker. Make another mark 4 inches ahead of the stock marks, then re-hang the string. This is the new altered wheelbase front axle centerline. Use the string frequently to ensure equal spindle positioning on each side of the car as the job progresses.

2 The stock front suspension parts weigh 138 pounds. Like many original Dart match racers (Billy Jacobs' Kid Goat, the Liberty Motors Corruptor's Pup, and the Esserman Dodge Rampage), the stock K-frame and aluminum manual steering box are retained.

3 With the stock stuff out of the way, work can begin. We will position the leaf springs directly beneath the stock frame rails, which are $30\frac{3}{4}$ inches apart, from center to center. Like most Chrysler unibodies, the Dart's front frame rails are parallel, a fact that greatly simplifies leaf spring installation.

4 In a perfect world we'd order a tubular-steel straight axle with disc brakes and custom leaf springs. But at about $1,900 as shown, we can save money by hitting the junkyard.

5 The Dodge A100 van front axle assembly was used under countless match racers and gassers back in the day, and it's still a valid choice. At 223 pounds, it's a heavy beast, but for a total junkyard cost of $242 (with springs and brakes), it's a budget saver. At $63\frac{1}{4}$ inches drum-to-drum, it is $7\frac{1}{4}$ inches wider than the Dart's stock track width—not good, but we can fix that. The spring pads are $36\frac{1}{4}$ inches apart versus the Dart's $30\frac{3}{4}$-inch rail-to-rail front frame width. By removing $5\frac{1}{2}$ inches from the center of the A100 van axle, the drum-to-drum distance drops to $57\frac{3}{4}$ inches (stock Dart is 56 drum to drum) and the space between the spring pads drops to $30\frac{3}{4}$ inches—our fitment problems are solved.

6 The Dodge A100 van leaf springs weigh $37\frac{1}{2}$ pounds each and are 46 inches long (unloaded). We'd be tempted to replace them with shorter springs if we didn't note their use on the Kid Goat, Corruptor's Pup, and Rampage altered wheelbase Darts from back in the day. Here, they are supported on jack stands so their axle location pins are exactly 4 inches forward from the stock Dart position as confirmed by the weighted string. Notice how the leading ends of the springs and the shackles protrude beyond the ends of the Dart frame rails. Simple frame extensions will solve that. Remember, the longer the spring, the smoother the ride.

RAMPAGE DART CONSTRUCTION OVERVIEW

The ends of the frame extensions are capped with welded steel plates. Dale also supplemented all factory spot welds in the area with full seam welds for extra strength in this high-stress region.

To accommodate the long springs, 4-inch frame rail extensions were cut from 2½-inch square tubing and welded to the frame ends. Then, 1¼-inch tubular sleeves were welded to them to accept the rubber shackle bushings. The A100 van springs flatten and gain 2 inches of length (for a total of 48 inches) when fully loaded. If you don't compensate for this and weld everything in place with unloaded springs, the spring shackles may bind.

With the springs in their final position, the frame is marked and a pair of rear spring mounts are fashioned from 3 x 3-inch square tubing with 1/2-inch holes drilled for the spring-eye through-bolts. The spring mounts are then welded to both sides of the Dart's frame, taking care to ensure that they are exactly aligned. This prevents a cock-eyed axle installation.

Now it's time to narrow the axle to suit the Dart's tighter dimensions by removing 5½ inches from its width. A reciprocating saw makes quick work of the forged-steel axle beam. Cutting torches are not recommended as they are not precise enough for this job and leave rough edges.

With fresh MP rubber spring-eye bushings installed, here's what it looks like when the springs are installed. Note that the shackle is perpendicular to the ground as the spring hangs free. When the springs are compressed with a full vehicle load, the bottom of the shackle juts forward and assumes the desired 30- to 45-degree angle for proper function without binding.

Here's a look at the severed axle. We're going through the trouble of removing 5½ inches because the 63½ inch stock width would push the front wheels out too far and look strange. Aesthetics count as much as function. The 5½-inch-width reduction also brings the axle's integral spring pads into perfect alignment with the Dart's frame rails and puts them directly under the leaf spring center pins for simplified installation.

HOW TO BUILD ALTERED WHEELBASE CARS

CHAPTER 3

13 Before welding, Dale uses an abrasive disc to grind deep chamfers into the ends of the axle beam. This creates a valley when they're butted together and ensures deep weld penetration for maximum strength.

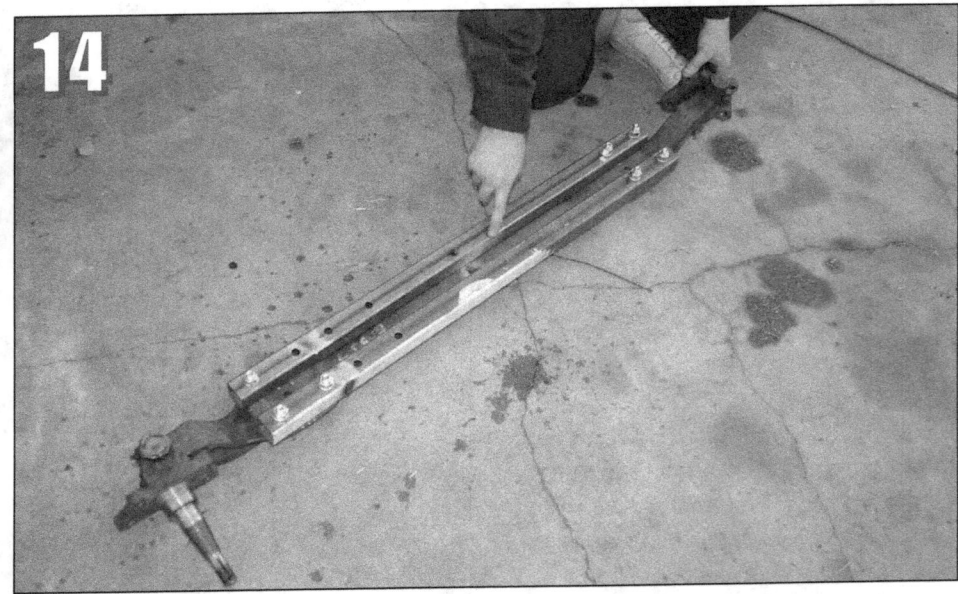

14 Dale made this rigid fixture from square tubing to keep the axle halves perfectly aligned as they're welded back together. If the segments shift, king pin alignment, caster, and camber can be disturbed and cause spooky handling, steering hassles, and uneven tire wear. Dale's fixture ensures perfect alignment from start to finish.

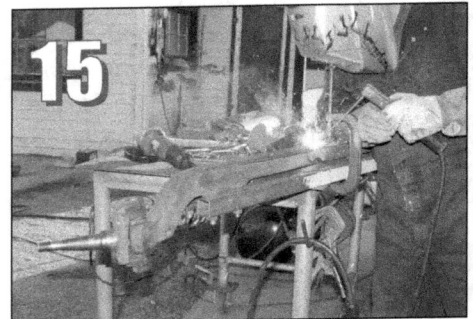

15 Unlike the modern MIG weld technique used on the rest of the Dart, good old-fashioned arc welding is used to rejoin the axle beam. Arc welding offers highly localized heat for excellent flow of the molten metal for the best union.

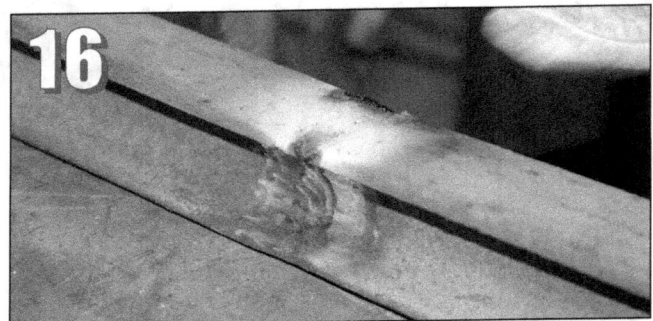

16 The weld must be allowed to cool naturally before it is ground smooth. Never force the issue by splashing with water, as thermal shock can degrade the strength of the weld.

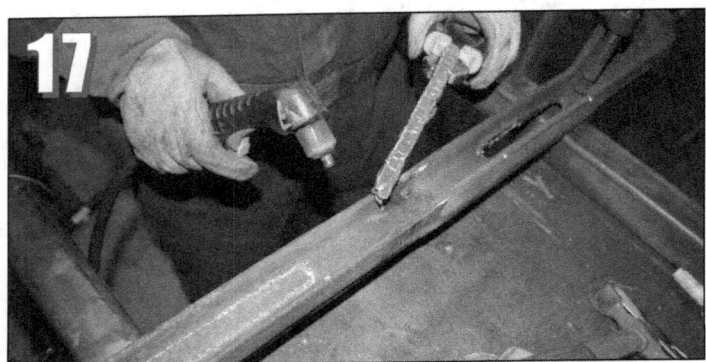

17 Two 6-inch slots were cut into the axle beam using a plasma cutter. Lots of A100-equipped funny cars—most notably Mr. Norm's 8-second supercharged Hemi Coronet, featured slotted axle beams. We cut them more for appearance than any tangible weight savings.

18 Here's the preliminary installation. Pretty basic, huh? The most critical detail is maintaining exact parallelism and symmetry of execution from side to side. Frequent checking with the weighted string confirms the correct axle centerline position as work proceeds.

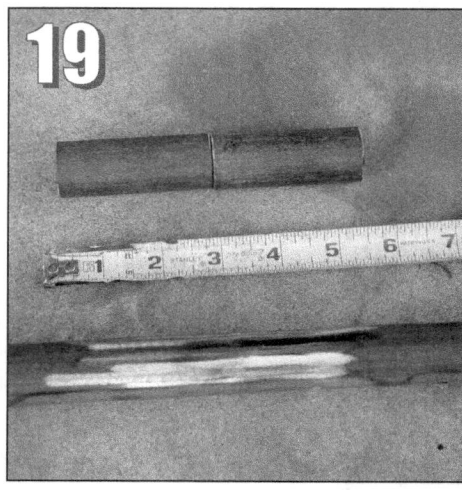

The stock A100 steering tie rod is reused after a 5½-inch section is removed to match the new axle width.

To preserve critical strength in the shortened tie rod, a steel sleeve made of 1/16-inch-thick, 3/4-inch round tube was inserted prior to welding the halves together. Small holes are drilled in the tie rod and filled with plug welds to keep the inner sleeve from moving.

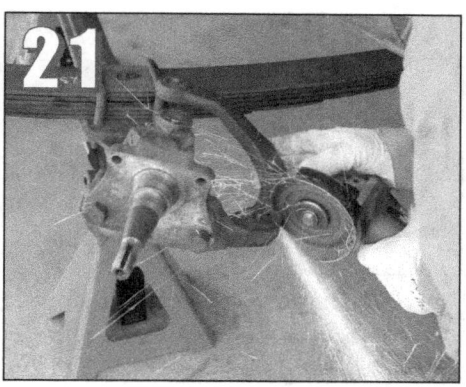

The process of connecting the Dart's steering box to the front wheels took some trial and error. We started by cutting the stock A100 van steering arm extension off the driver-side spindle. Some straight-axle installers run a simple link from the steering box to the driver-side front wheel (Mr. Norm's 165-mph blown Coronet was one of them) for a near-steer solution. That's an invitation for bump steer where potholes (and extreme body rise during drag strip launches) send feedback to the steering wheel, and spooky handling results. This Dart is a street and strip machine so we'll go with the cross-steer method.

As noted in the section on the construction of the Wilshire Shaker Nova, the term cross-steer simply refers to the fact that the steering box sends inputs to the passenger-side wheel via a long drag link. This setup reduces bump steer. To get the benefit of cross-steering, the A100 steering arm extension was transferred to the passenger-side spindle and tack welded in place while we figured out the required drag link configuration. My finger points to the weld at the end of the extension, where one of the Dart's original spindle arm ends was attached.

Here's a look at the customized, passenger-side steering knuckle configuration prior to final welding. As with most beam axle designs, these knuckles bolt to the spindles, greatly easing the welding process.

Note that temporary tack welds hold everything together until the real welds replace them. As on the forged-steel axle beam, the steering knuckle unions must be deeply chamfered with the grinder before the arc welder is used to fill them. After welding it's just as durable as a one-piece forging.

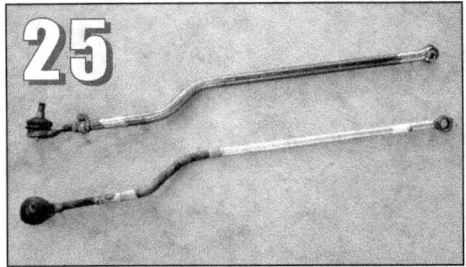

The drag link took a few tries before we got good oil-pan clearance and proper steering travel, so Dale whipped up a series of temporary test parts from thin-wall electrical conduit (foreground). Once the final shape was arrived at, a thick-wall .85-inch-diameter steel tubing drag link was made. At the steering box end (right), the circular end of the stock Dart steering link was welded on for compatibility with the stock Dart pitman arm. At the other end, one of the Dart's stock sleeve adjusters was welded to the end of the new drag link for an added measure of adjustability.

All parts are raw and unpainted for now but we'll sand blast everything and apply paint and detailing later on.

Sharing their 11 x 3-inch dimensions with the brakes used on Mopar Street Hemi muscle cars, the massive A-100 drum brakes will easily handle the 130-mph trap speed. At 38 pounds each they aren't light, but the price is right.

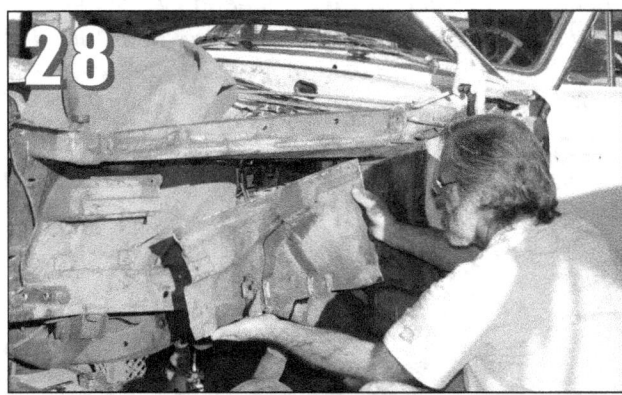

With the stock upper control arms sitting in the scrap bin, the inner fender aprons (and their control arm mounts) were removed with the plasma cutter. A set of wild spaghetti headers will soon run through this area and let the Max-Wedge breathe.

Stock Dart shock absorbers bolt to the A100 axle, but upper shock mounts need to be fabricated from steel plate. Make sure the shock absorber is half compressed with the spring fully loaded before welding the top mounts in place.

The 4-inch axle centerline relocation creates tire contact with the BF Goodrich 6.00-15-inch Silvertown bias-ply skins and 15 x 4.5-inch Torq-Thrust Ds. Two possible remedies exist. One is to slice the wheel opening away from the fender and slide it forward 4 inches, then fill the gaps using the same technique employed on the Dart's rear quarter panels. The trouble is that the Dart's fender shapes are too complex for graceful results. The other tactic is to simply trim away metal until clearance is gained.

RAMPAGE DART CONSTRUCTION OVERVIEW

With a vintage photo of Gene Snow's Rambunctious *injected Hemi Dart match racer for guidance, Dale used a plasma cutter and disc grinder to trim the fender for tire clearance. This same tactic was employed on the* Rampage, Kid Goat, *and* Corruptor's Pup *Dart match racers, so we're in good company.*

Final tuning of fender clearance is performed with tin snips and a careful eye. It's always a good idea to mock up things several times before sending any car to the paint shop.

The plasma cutter is used to notch the front valance panel for spring shackle clearance.

The finished job looks great and is period correct. Thanks to the 5½-inch axle width reduction, the 57¾-inch front track is perfect. Note how the bottoms of the laden shackles jut out at the desired 30 degrees from perpendicular. Follow our work and you'll also get 8 degrees of positive caster for excellent steering-return characteristics. About 1/4 inch of toe-in keeps the tires from wandering. Sure, the A100 axle swap added 85 pounds of mostly un-sprung weight, but the effect on the Dart's weight distribution (45/55)—and stance—is worth it. Now we're ready for the Max-Wedge!

Up to this point, the Dart's stock Slant Six and push-button 904 Torqueflite transmission were in place. But now we're ready to swap in a Max-Wedge. We added 100 pounds of ballast each time we checked ride height to simulate the extra mass of the big-block V-8.

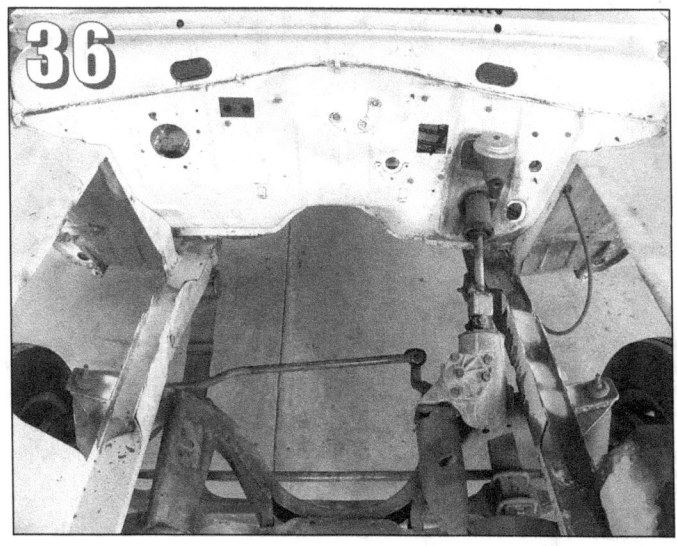

Here's a final look at the completed steering layout. Note that the drag link is contoured to provide oil pan clearance.

HOW TO BUILD ALTERED WHEELBASE CARS

CHAPTER 3

Install Engine and Transmission

1. The only correct choice for propulsion is a Max-Wedge or a Hemi. Small-blocks simply were not used by match racers back in the day and greatly dilute the full impact of a modern Match Bash tribute car. Since the original Rampage started out with a Max-Wedge—and knowing a 426 Hemi would break the bank—we'll go for the Wedge. Though real Max-Wedge parts are extremely expensive, we can get pretty close with a basic 440. We pulled this group of 440s from motor homes at the local Pick-A-Part recycling yard. At $163.44 each (the flat rate for any V-8) we couldn't stop at just one.

2. All of the 440s were running engines, so we randomly pulled one aside for rebuilding. It's a standard-bore piece with a 1977 casting date.

3. Schumacher Creative Services offers this kit to swap a Chrysler big-block into a 1963–1966 A-body. The V-8 bolts directly to the Slant Six K-frame with only minor trimming to clear the oil pump and filter. All parts are powdercoated and urethane isolators are used for maximum strength.

4. A cherry picker lowers the bare 440 block into the Dart for the very first time.

5. As advertised, the Schumacher mounts do a beautiful job of positioning the 440 block in a stock orientation. A stock oil pan will make contact with the Dart's small K-frame, but the problem is solved by using a Milodon 7-quart oil pan (PN MIL-31010). Its tidy mid-mounted sump clears the K-frame with room to spare.

HOW TO BUILD ALTERED WHEELBASE CARS

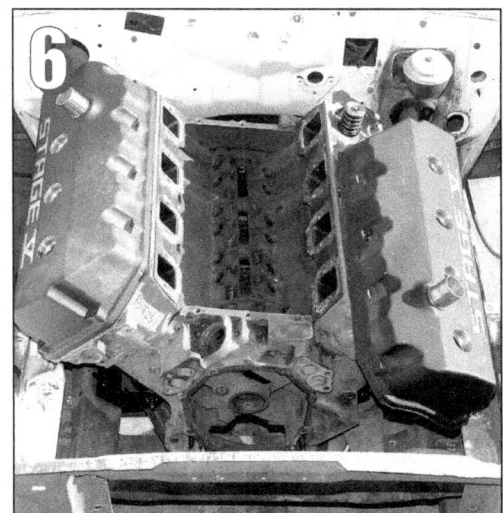

6 For kicks we placed a set of Hemi heads on the wedge block to see how they fit the car. The only major snag is where the stock master cylinder fights for space with the driver-side rocker cover. We'll stick with the Max-Wedge . . . for now.

7 The original 1962–1964 Max-Wedge big-blocks were serious machines with high-quality forged internals. On the other hand, 440s built after about 1972 have cast-iron crankshafts and are more about making torque than winning races. Still, our cast-crank 440 will easily produce enough power for respectable quarter-mile times. Superior Automotive handled the rebuild.

8 For easy cruising on 91-octane unleaded pump gas, engine assembler Scott Emley specified KB Silvolite cast hypereutectic pistons (PN KB146) that yield 9.75:1 compression. The Isky 292 Mega hydraulic flat-tappet cam (PN 165129) has .505/.505 lift and 244 degrees of duration at .050-inch lift.

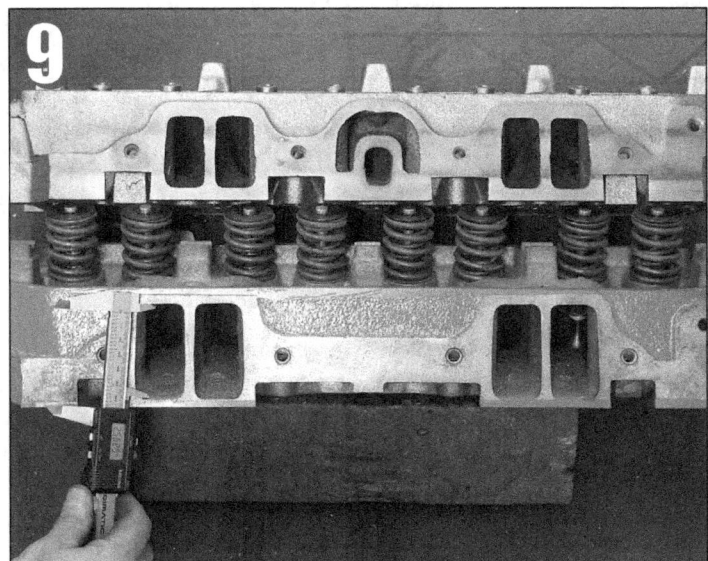

9 Original 1962–1964 Max-Wedge heads (bottom) have massive intake and exhaust ports but are very rare today. Though reproductions are now available, we'll stick with the stock 440 motorhome heads to preserve the budget. Their port volumes may be 20 percent smaller than the Max-Wedge, but their 2.08-/1.74-inch-diameter valves are fully capable of supporting 500 hp without porting. Notice the exhaust-heat crossover passage on the 440 heads.

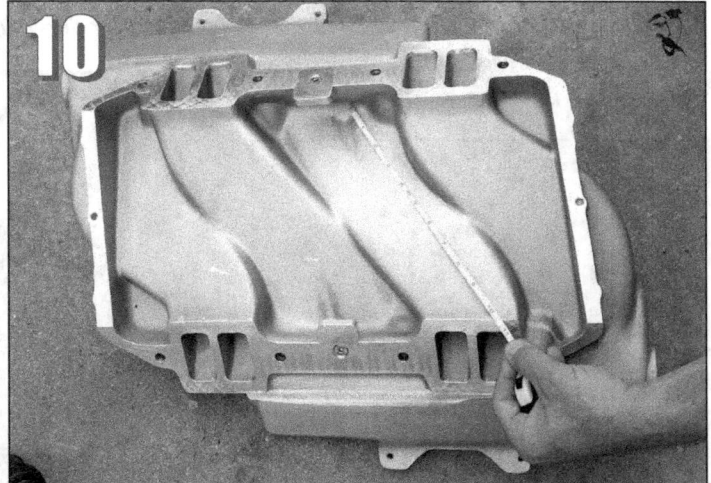

10 Single carburetors are too tame for a proper Match Bash car; we must have a Max-Wedge cross ram or it just isn't right. Until recently we'd have been forced to step up to expensive Max-Wedge heads. But since A&A released this reproduction Max-Wedge cross ram with smaller 440 port openings (PN RMWACRIM-14), owners of mundane 440s can enjoy a cross ram without changing heads. The A&A plenum volumes and 11-inch runners are identical to original Max-Wedge specifications, but aluminum inserts block the unnecessary exhaust-heat crossover passage.

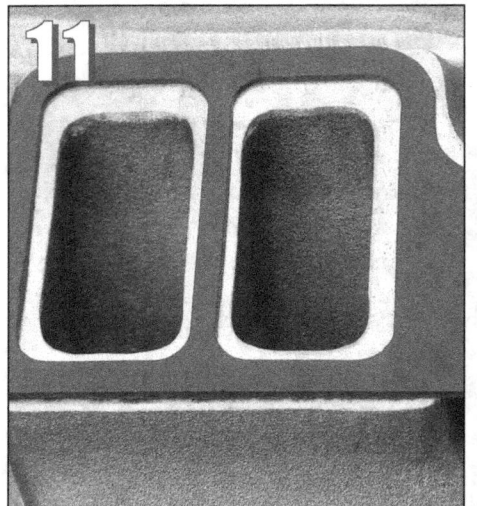

An original Max-Wedge intake manifold gasket highlights the smaller size of the 440 ports cast into the A&A cross ram. Yes, we'll leave some power on the table but the extra 14 ci provided by using the 440 short-block makes up for some of it. A&A also offers Max-Wedge cross rams with the original big ports as well as cross rams for 426 Hemi applications for Match Bash builders with deeper pockets than ours.

On the Superior Automotive dyno, the 440-based Max-Wedge clone belts out 436 hp at 5,500 rpm and 491.2 ft-lbs at 4,100 rpm. Dual Edelbrock 500-cfm carburetors (PN 1404) supply the gas. The Mancini Racing reproduction Max-Wedge exhaust manifolds (PN 413426440) are beautiful but will be replaced by custom fenderwell headers in the car.

Fresh off the dyno, the burly mill is ready for installation. It just wouldn't look the same with a mundane single carburetor, would it? Exotic induction is a key element of any successful Match Bash creation, regardless of make.

The vast majority of match racers relied on the mighty Chrysler 727 Torqueflite automatic transmission. Introduced in 1962, several years before GM and Ford announced competitive automatic transmissions, the 727 was also a favorite among non-Mopar racers. The Torqueflite-equipped Wilshire Shaker Chevy Nova is a prime example.

An empty case eases trial installation. Though the transmission is bolted to the engine, contact with the transmission tunnel prevents installation of the transmission crossmember.

RAMPAGE DART CONSTRUCTION OVERVIEW

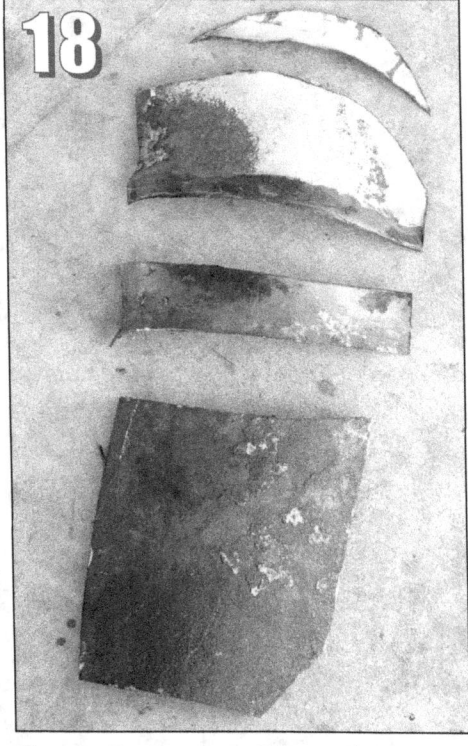

The 1963–1966 Dart floorpan was designed to accept the smaller 904 Torqueflite transmission. The big 727 hits the firewall and transmission tunnel in several places.

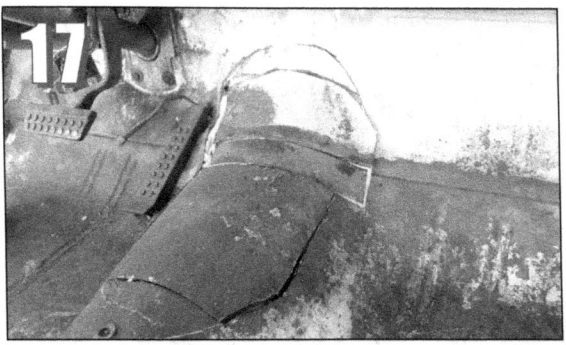

Inside, the small transmission tunnel is apparent. In 1967 Chrysler redesigned the A-body (Dart, Valiant, Barracuda) to accept the big 727, but that doesn't help us. We need to rework the transmission tunnel. Here, a series of slices have been made with a circular cut-off wheel.

For clarity, here are the sections.

With the offending metal out of the way, the 727 can be lifted up so the transmission crossmember can be installed for support. A larger transmission tunnel can be fabricated from sheet steel and welded in place.

The stock transmission crossmember is designed to accept only the smaller rubber transmission mount used in 904 applications. The corners (marked in white paint) must be trimmed for the larger 727 transmission mount to fit.

HOW TO BUILD ALTERED WHEELBASE CARS

A series of intersecting plunge cuts eliminates the offending metal.

The modified crossmember is ready to accept the 727 transmission mount. We used a polyurethane mount from Imperial Services. It's stronger than the original rubber type and is impervious to damage from fluid leaks.

Push-button transmission controls are a huge bonus in any Torqueflite-equipped Match Bash car since they were so popular back in the day. To get them you need to use a 1962–1965 cable-operated transmission, which has the transmission mount bolts spaced 4 inches apart. Later 1966-up 727s (left) were redesigned and have $2^{13}/_{16}$ inches between the mounting fasteners. If you use the later Torqueflite in an early A- or B-body Mopar you'll need to address this with some custom fabrication. All pre-1967 727s have a specific 19-spline input shaft that requires a matched torque converter. Later 1967-up 24-spline converters will not properly engage the splines of a stock 1962–1966 727. If you swap a later 24-spline input shaft and matching reaction shaft support into an early 727, you'll be able to choose from a huge selection of modern high-stall torque converters.

The 1962–1964 727 output shaft has a circular companion flange (right) and mates to a ball-and-trunion-style drive shaft. In 1965-up Chrysler switched to a conventional splined output shaft (left) and slip-yolk-style drive shaft. Both styles are fully capable of handling 800 hp. A 1964 Plymouth Belvedere driveshaft was shortened to $41^{1}/_{2}$ inches to suit the Dart's reduced wheelbase.

25. The stock 19-inch Slant Six radiator has two rows and will not keep the big block cool; also, the lower hose nipple is positioned on the wrong side for compatibility. A custom high-efficiency aluminum radiator is one possible solution.

26. We'll use a 22-inch-wide radiator from a 1967 Dart. Though the lower mounting bolts are positioned lower, re-drilling the holes in the radiator wall solve the problem. Re-cored with a 4-row copper core, the new radiator keeps coolant temperature below 190 degrees and looks like the stock radiator used in the original *Rampage Dart*. The cooling system capacity is 3½ gallons.

27. A small amount of trimming opens the radiator wall so the new radiator gets full air flow. An engine driven 7-blade Chrysler 17½-inch-diameter fan is only 1¼ inches thick and provides plenty of airflow at low speed.

28. The 3,500-rpm Art Carr torque converter offers a good mix of street cruising efficiency and flash-stall to compliment the nearly 500 ft-lbs of torque on hand. A B&M auxiliary transmission fluid cooler (PN 70268) keeps operating temperature under 180 degrees for long transmission life.

CHAPTER 3

Install Hood Scoop

1 Borrowing a page from the 1963–1964 Max-Wedge B-body program we use aluminum velocity stacks to channel cold air from the hood scoop to the dual Edelbrock 500s. But how do we know where to cut the holes in the hood? It all starts by pulling strings across the tops of the carburetors with the ends firmly taped to the car. We mark the metal at the side of each string where it is taped to the car to serve as reference points so they can be removed and reattached in the same position.

2 The strings must intersect directly above the air cleaner studs. While the front clip of the Dart is removed, you can do the job on a complete car by just opening and closing the hood. Just be sure to make the strings long enough to compensate for the added height of the closed hood.

3 The stock underhood bracing interferes with the Max-Wedge air cleaners and also sits directly in the cut path. We need smooth underhood surfaces to merge with the foam velocity stack seals; with a little help from the cut off wheel, it's history. The 1963 and 1964 factory Max-Wedge B-bodies are also devoid of this bracing for the same reason.

4 Now, un-stick one end of each string and bolt the hood in place (or close it, as the case may be). With the hood situated, pull the stings back over the hood skin and re-stick them using the marked lines to ensure they still intersect directly above the carburetor studs.

5 Here's another view of how the strings look when properly placed on the hood.

RAMPAGE DART CONSTRUCTION OVERVIEW

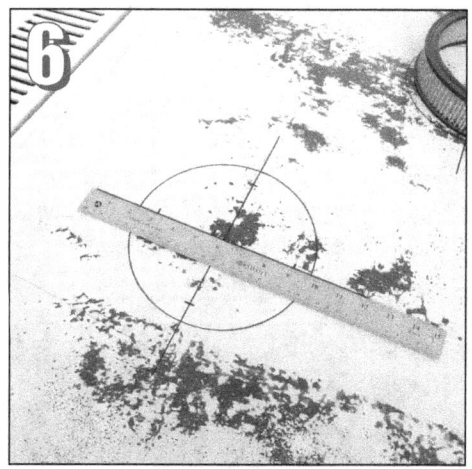

Use a straightedge and felt-tip marker to indicate where the strings intersect onto the hood skin. Extend the lines 10 inches out from the intersection points. Remember, the driver-side carburetor is staggered ahead of the passenger-side carburetor on a Max-Wedge cross ram. Don't get confused and mark the wrong intersections!

A perfectly centered 8-inch air filter element makes a great stencil for marking the hood skin for cutting. Use the inside diameter of the filter so the hole is 7½ inches across.

After covering the engine and carburetors with heavy plastic sheeting to prevent contamination from grit and metal debris, make a plunge cut with a cut-off wheel to breach the hood skin.

A second slice opens a triangular area large enough to gain access for tin shears. Although the cut-off wheel is great for slicing in straight lines and gradual curves, it's not so good at making tight circular cuts and will leave a crunchy result. Not recommended.

Tin shears are sold in three varieties for straight cuts, left-hand cuts, and right-hand cuts. I'm right-handed so I used the left-hand shears to cut the holes in a counter-clockwise direction. Take small bites so you can more accurately "steer" the shears and get a clean circular hole rather than a jagged mess. You'll notice that as you cut, the severed hood skin binds up and impedes progress. The solution is to simply pry it up and out of the way in small sections and then keep cutting. Use care not to apply leverage or prying force on the "good side" of the hood skin; that would distort it and force corrective bodywork later.

HOW TO BUILD ALTERED WHEELBASE CARS

CHAPTER 3

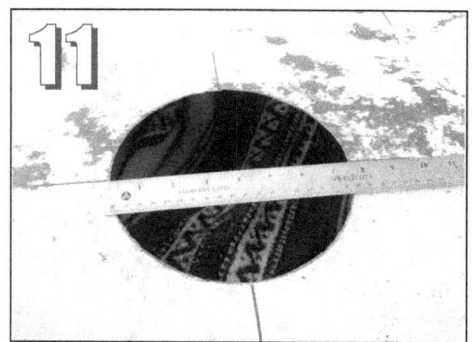

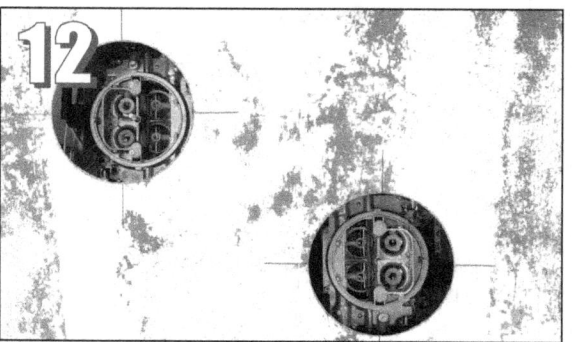

So how close did our "blind" marking and cutting technique come to hitting the mark? This bird's-eye view shows we got it spot-on. Looking straight down, notice how the marked lines are in exact alignment with the air cleaner stud. It doesn't get any better than this.

The finished holes measure 7 1/2 inches. While reproduction spun-aluminum B-body Max-Wedge velocity stacks are available from outfits like Kramer Automotive Specialties, we're betting they don't fit a hybrid combination like this Max-Wedge-powered early A-body. The concern is that the distance from the carburetor flange to the underside of the hood skin differs from a factory-spec B-body Max-Wedge car. As such, the foam ring seals on the B-body velocity stacks may—or may not—be tall enough to reach the Dart's hood. Instead, we'll use a set of generic 8-inch air cleaner bases (non-drop style) and make our own foam seals to suit the required height.

Now that the hood has a pair of Max-Wedge-style holes in it, we need to cover it with an appropriate scoop.

Original Max-Wedge hood scoops were made of lightweight aluminum and Jim Kramer can sell you a beautiful reproduction if your wallet is deep enough. For us, a fiberglass replica—also from Kramer—does the trick.

The amazing thing is how the stock 1963 Dart hood doesn't hit the Max-Wedge—even with the air cleaners in place! This means we can cruise the street with filtered air or feed the dual quads through the hood scoop by swapping to open-velocity stacks at the strip. If we hadn't eliminated the under-hood bracing, none of this would be possible. Despite the lack of bracing, the hood is still very rigid.

Build Fenderwell Headers

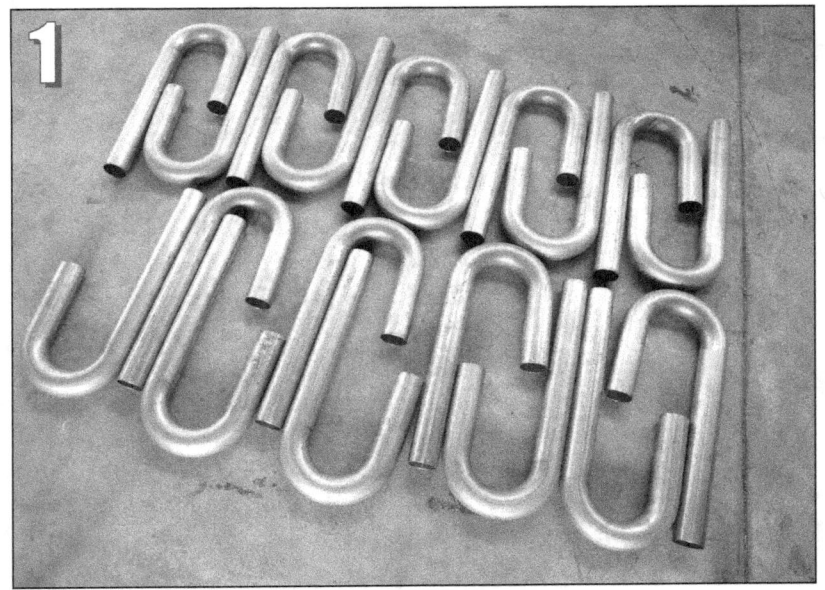

1. We don't have a $600 tubing bender, so we used eleven 2-inch J-bends from Summit for a cost of $165 (PN SUM-621005, $14.95 each). Made from 16-gauge mandrel-bent steel tubing, they're thick and last a long time. The beauty of J-bends is their versatility. By slicing and rotating sections of the tube, you can match the results of a tubing bender, and since each J-bend can yield three to five useful pieces, there's virtually zero waste. Primary header tube diameter (and length) affects the RPM at which the engine's torque peak occurs. Generally speaking, the smaller the diameter, the lower the torque peak, and vice versa. Our 440 will thrive with 2-inch pipes. We also paid $20 for 8 feet of 2-inch straight tubing from a local muffler shop to span the gaps between the curved sections.

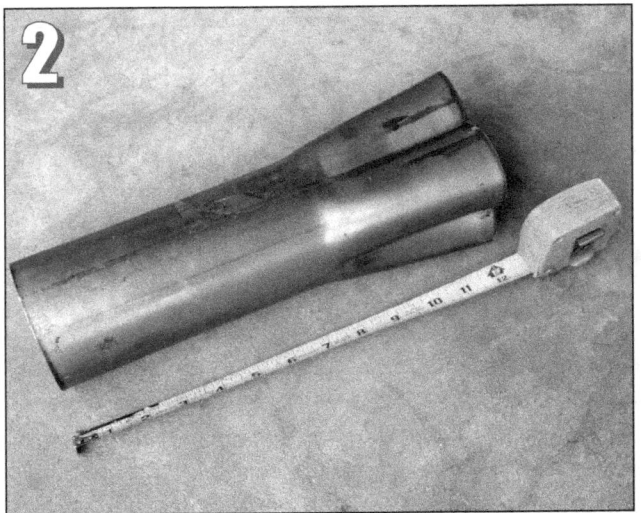

2. Collector volume capacity affects low-RPM torque and is an area that's been well researched. Generally, the larger the capacity, the more torque you get. We got a set of Hedman collectors from Summit (HED-14015) for $42.99. They're 12 inches long and merge the 2-inch primary tubes into a common 3½-inch-diameter plenum.

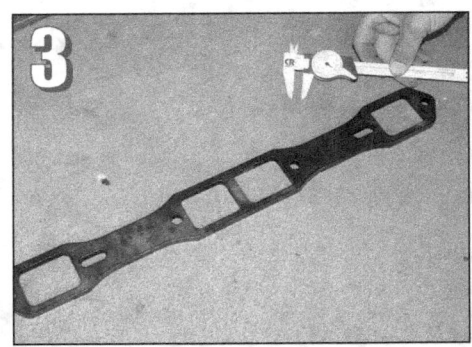

3. AVH Technology sells beefy 3/8-inch-thick laser-cut big-block Mopar header flanges. Avoid chintzy stamped steel flanges unless you like the sound of blown header gaskets.

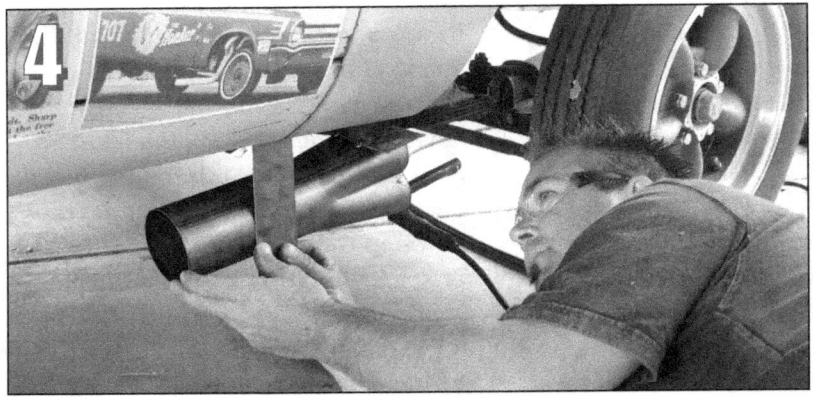

4. Ace fabricator Dale "Can Do" Kutsch gets started by positioning the collector where it looks best and tack welding it in place with scrap steel supports. Because proper fenderwell headers must be visible for maximum in-your-face value, they need to be prominently displayed immediately below the rockers. Note the vintage picture of Bud Faubel's *Honker* SS/A 1964 Dodge taped to the door. Use a vintage photo as your guide for best results.

CHAPTER 3

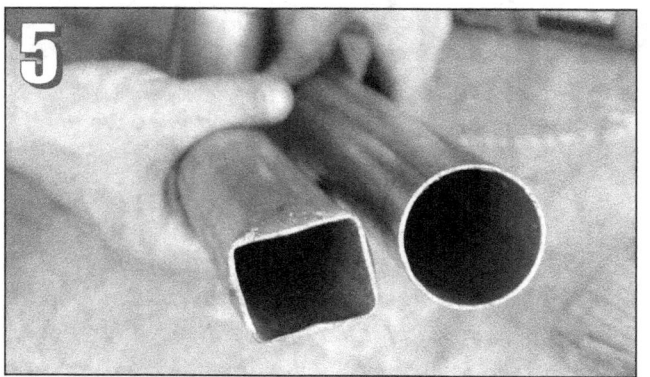

To get the round primary tubes to fit into the rectangular flanges, Dale simply uses a wooden block. With the tube set against the cement floor, he taps it gently for a few minutes to reshape the end.

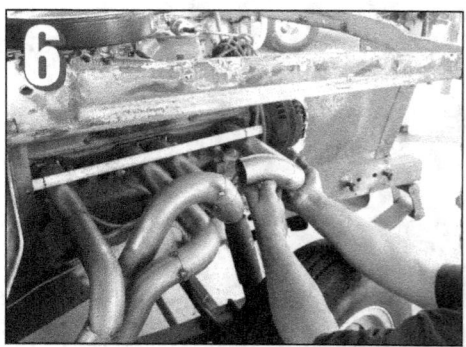

Working one tube at a time, Dale tack welds a length of tube to the header flange so it shoots straight out. The outward and downward flow continues with the addition of a second tube, its end trimmed to establish a downward trajectory. Notice the white steel bar placed across the header tubes. It serves as a guide to make sure the tubes remain aligned during construction.

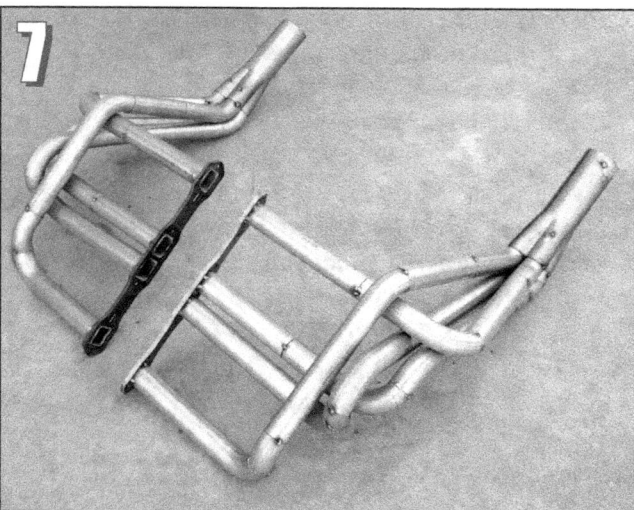

Prior to final seam welding. These headers are loosely patterned after the Mark III Max-Wedge headers sold by the Ramchargers in 1964. The primary tubes range in length from 35 to 50 inches. Although equal-length primaries are the ideal for cylinder scavenging, we'll still get plenty of power from the mill.

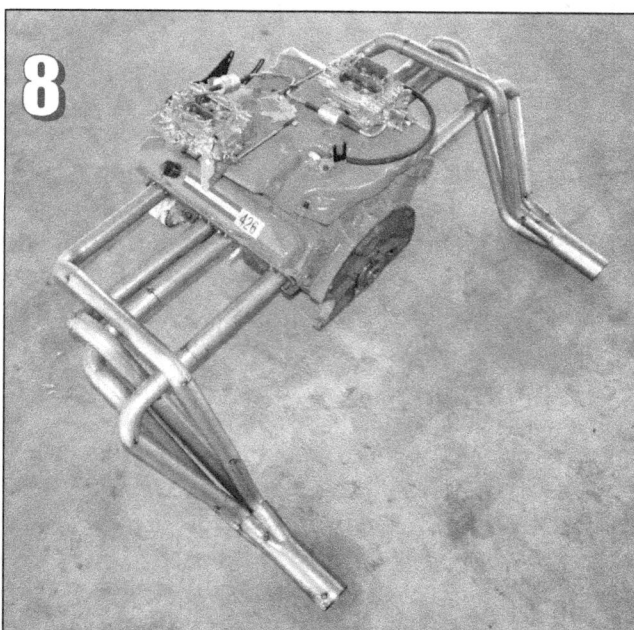

Running straight out the side of each cylinder head, fender-well headers are free from the hassle of having to clear steering linkage and frame members below the engine. Not shown here are the welded collector flanges and bolt-on caps so we can cork it for street driving. Dale added a pair of 2½-inch outlets to the inboard side of each collector that merge with an under-car dual-exhaust system and high-capacity mufflers.

In the old days, rusty headers were inevitable and high-temperature header paint was the only protection. Today we can do better. Young Gun Performance Coatings treated the headers to this white ceramic coating. Young Gun's Carlos Baldomero uses a spray gun to apply the pigmented liquid compound. Then, the headers go into Young Gun's garage-size oven and bake for an hour at 500 degrees F. Young Gun gets $300 to coat a set of spider-leg headers and welcomes your special projects. Young Gun also offers silver, titanium, black, red, and blue colors.

RAMPAGE DART CONSTRUCTION OVERVIEW

Apply Body Graphics and Lettering

Match Bash cars should have all side trim removed so it doesn't conflict with the application of graphics and lettering. Weld the mounting holes closed using a MIG welder set for low heat to minimize panel distortion.

The Dart looks a little bland all dressed in white, so let's spruce it up with some period graphics. The cool checkerboard roof pattern used on Jack Sharkey's Esserman Dodge-sponsored *Rampage* 1964 Dart match racer will guide us.

The original *Rampage* was initially built with a standard wheelbase, 426 Max-Wedge and Chrysler A833 4-speed manual transmission. It was eventually transformed into this altered wheelbase match racer with a 426 Race Hemi running a cross ram, and then Hilborn fuel injection. The current whereabouts of this wicked car are unknown. (Rampage Collection)

After studying numerous vintage photos of the *Rampage*, it looks like each checker measures about 6 inches square. The job starts with finding the vehicle centerline and marking it onto the roof. Measuring out 3 inches from each side of the centerline gives the width of the first 6 x 6-inch checker, which will be white (or body color). From this centered square, we now work outward and mark the roof every 6 inches to establish the widths of the alternating colored squares. Note that we've marked the roof "B" for black and "W" for white to avoid confusion as the work progresses.

HOW TO BUILD ALTERED WHEELBASE CARS

The roof of a car is not like a table top. It has compound curves, is not a perfect square, and is not perfectly flat, so the width of the squares around the borders of the pattern must be reduced to fit. The length, however, must remain constant at 6 inches or the intersection of the black and white squares loses alignment and the effect is ruined. Note how the inner border of the squares is razor straight and perfectly aligned while the edges that border the drip rail are allowed to conform to its shape. With careful measuring and marking based on fixed reference points on the body, these exact same outlines are applied to the opposite side of the roof panel.

At the top of the C-pillar, some finessing is required. The trick is to progressively compress the height of the squares in this row to preserve the alignment of the pattern on the roof top while accommodating the horizontal lines established on the C-pillar. This curved transition in the roof skin from horizontal to vertical is the best place to trick the eye into ignoring the compressed squares so they don't stand out from the rest of the pattern. Note how the height of the upper row of checkers is tapered while the second and third rows retain the strict 6 x 6-inch discipline. The sections to be painted black are indicated with a marker and the white sections are indicated with an erasable pencil.

Moving toward the rear of the car, the pattern is extended, but the height of the squares is reduced to conform to the borders defined by the body lines and sheetmetal contours.

With the squares marked off, mask each one with tape and begin applying paint following the appropriate black-white-black-white alternating pattern. We used Dupli-Color semi-gloss black acrylic enamel. This rattle-can strategy delivers great backyard results that last for years.

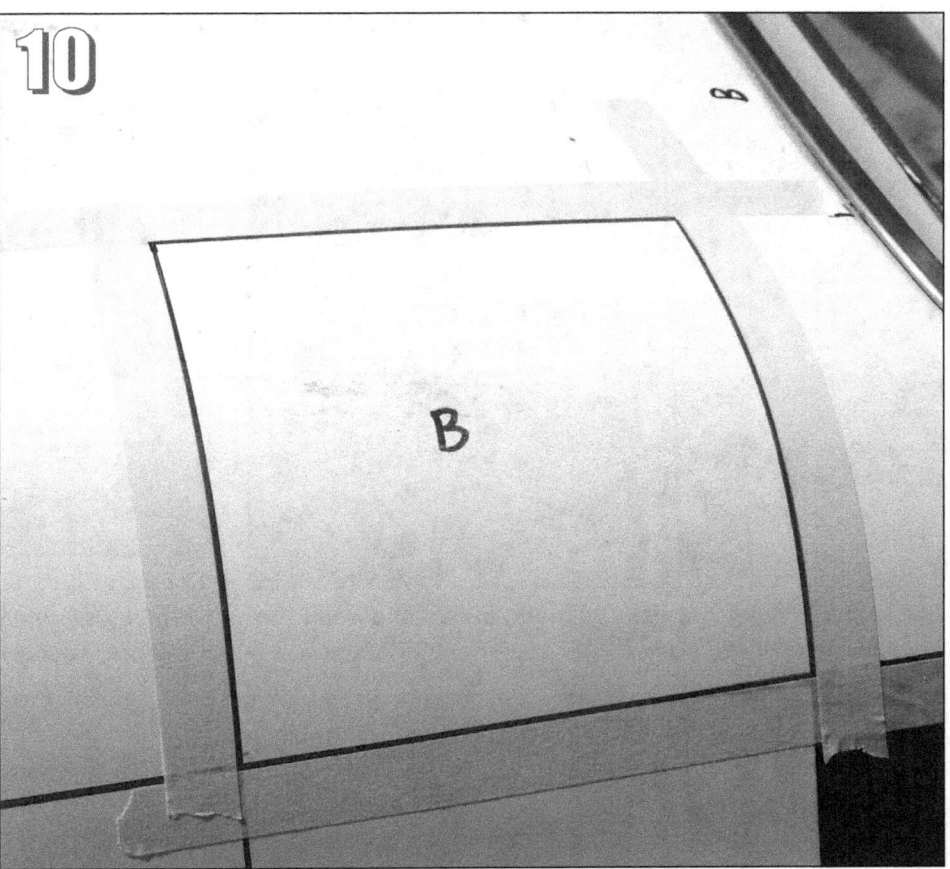

Continue masking and spraying the black squares, making sure to apply the tape to the outside edge of the border markings—not the inside edge. This prevents the squares from being undersize and failing to "connect" at the corners with the white squares. Note how the height of this row of squares tapers as it reaches the rear of the roof. Again, it's a crafty way of fooling the eye. The pattern has to be compressed somewhere to fit the roof. This is the best place to do it.

Here's a close-up of the proper masking approach for each black square. Note how the tape border is outside the square to be painted. Newspaper or similar material is applied to the perimeter of the tape around each square to avoid overspray.

One square at a time, the pattern begins to take shape. Working in the hot California sun makes the enamel paint dry in minutes and allows fast progress. Let the sun heat the can so the paint flows better.

With the tricky C-pillars finished, paint the first black square at the leading edge of the roof skin and work your way back. Remember to keep that inner border arrow straight so the pattern doesn't wander off course.

The same technique is used to mark, mask, and paint the opposite side of the body.

Thanks to careful measurements, the sides of the car are perfectly symmetrical. This takes care of the vertical surfaces; now what about the roof?

Applying the pattern to the horizontal surface of the roof skin is easier than doing the vertical sides of the car, but the unforgiving nature of the delicate interlock between the black and white squares calls for careful planning before applying a drop of paint. Like the leading edge of the roof skin, the vehicle centerline is established and marked atop the back window. Then the 6-inch-wide squares are plotted outward from there.

Bright pink surveyor's string is taped to the longitudinal borders of the roof squares and pulled all the way back to the borders marked at the rear of the roof.

RAMPAGE DART CONSTRUCTION OVERVIEW

Here's how the strings look at the rear of the roof. If you've done the math correctly and taken plenty of time to work slowly, the distance between the strings should measure 6 inches any place you measure. If it doesn't, isolate the problem and make corrections before going further. Don't bank on fudging a few squares oversize or undersize, it'll stand out loud, clear, and ugly in the finished job.

The next step is to stretch strings width-wise across the roof every 6 inches to see if the grid is correctly envisioned. Again, if everything is correct, every square—except for the ones around the perimeter of the design—will measure exactly 6 x 6 inches.

The size of the roof skin prevents many of the squares from being full size, so make them shorter. One word on "good design": Always try to apply the pattern so the full-size 6 x 6-inch squares dominate the middle of the roof. Then surround them with the compressed squares. The side rows will be symmetric but there may be a difference in the size of leading and trailing rows. Always put the larger-size row of reduced squares in the lead—above the windshield. This is more appealing to the subconscious mind's eye.

The strings are used to confirm that the design is competent, symmetrical, and attractive. Before removal, mark the intersections of the strings with "+" signs. Then connect them with a steel ruler and pencil. Again, each square should measure 6 x 6 inches except for the compressed squares around the border. To prevent painting foul-ups, use an erasable pencil to mark each square B (for black) or W (for white).

HOW TO BUILD ALTERED WHEELBASE CARS

With all the squares marked off, begin painting the black ones using the same masking strategy used on the vertical surfaces. Work one square at a time. Don't rush.

As we paint our way across the roof, our careful preparation work pays dividends in the form of perfectly symmetric squares that merge gracefully at all four corners.

The finished job is a dead ringer for the effect used on the original Rampage. Sure, some may say this was a waste of time, considering that the car will be stripped down to bare metal later for a professional body and paint makeover. But until then, the car looks way cooler and we've had a great dress rehearsal for when we apply the real checkerboard pattern in the spray booth.

When it comes to graphics for modern Match Bash cars, avoid using copyrighted trademark names such as Ramchargers, Sox & Martin, Color Me Gone, etc. It is illegal and it does a disservice to the real car. But in the case of the Jack Sharkey's Rampage, his daughter's permission and enthusiasm for our tribute sets us free. Ace brush man Bob Thompson tapes blown-up images of the original Rampage to the Dart's flanks for inspiration.

RAMPAGE DART CONSTRUCTION OVERVIEW

Bob makes house calls, so his truck is always loaded with plenty of One Shot oil-based sign paint, brushes, and other tools of the trade. A professional race car lettering guy for more than 40 years, Bob has applied graphics to fabled cars like Al "Mousie" Marcellus' Winged Express *fuel altered reconstruction*, John Peters' Freight Train *dual-engine rail dragster*, as well as the Wilshire Shaker *Match Bash Nova*.

He starts the treatment by drawing each graphic element on a paper pattern that's taped to the side of the car. Here's the Esserman Dodge logo for the door.

Once the design is established, it is removed and placed on a soft table. Then a ponce wheel is used to perforate the outline of each graphic element. These pattern sheets will be used on both sides of the car to ensure symmetry—the mark of a professional.

After the ponce wheel treatment, the graphic pattern is re-taped to the car making sure it is perfectly horizontal and correctly positioned. Then a sock filled with blue chalk dust is patted over the image. This leaves a tracing of the design on the skin of the car. The paper is then removed so painting can begin. Remember to preserve the paper pattern for use on the other side of the body.

HOW TO BUILD ALTERED WHEELBASE CARS

CHAPTER 3

With the blue chalk outlines to serve as a guide, Bob applies horizontal tape-guide boundaries to ensure perfect horizontal margins. Now the paint work begins, using oil-based One Shot sign paint. Bob is an expert and can paint each letter freehand while maintaining consistent thickness and scale. Newcomers can achieve similar results simply by spending more time drawing the paper pattern before transferring it to the car with the chalk.

The same pattern–ponce–chalk process applies to the Rampage logo on the rear quarter panels. Although the original logo used an unusual reverse-italic treatment on the driver side (only) of the car, Bob says he never liked this style of font so he chose traditional forward-slanted italic letters.

Bob starts by filling the chalk outlines of each letter with black brush paint. Avoid air brushing as it delivers a too-smooth texture. Yes, we want to see the brush marks in the paint. Though you could substitute computer-cut vinyl graphics for paint, Bob says, "They're soul-less. That's the easy way out." We agree.

Because we couldn't find any color images of the original Rampage, we chose Insignia Red for the shadow treatment. Though many altered wheelbase funny car builders eliminated the stock gas-filler cap when they graduated to nitro and 5-gallon Moon tanks, the Rampage retained its stock 16-gallon fuel tank. Bob deftly blends the lettering to incorporate the removable filler cap.

RAMPAGE DART CONSTRUCTION OVERVIEW

Because early exposure to plastic model kits fueled my interest in drag racing and hot rods, let's honor the fact with a cool logo. This enlarged IMC logo was scanned off an original 1/25-scale Dodge L700 truck model kit box and enlarged several times on a color copy machine. The ponce wheel perforates the outline so it can be applied to the car.

Bob aligns the IMC logo on the front fender then tapes it down so the chalk bag can be used to transfer its outline onto the fender. We also thought about the JoHan logo as an alternate but the IMC checkerboard compliments the Dart's roof treatment perfectly.

Again, Bob used the chalk outline as a guide to fill the letters with black paint. The perimeter will be bordered with a thin red line to compliment the red shading on the Rampage logos. Little touches of tasteful, complementary shapes and matching colors unite the overall design of any graphics treatment.

As a nod to some of the great automotive journalists, Bob whipped up this mythical roster of helpers. You may recognize Roger Huntington, Alex Walordy, and Gray Baskerville for their many excellent magazine stories over the last four decades. Sadly, Roger and Gray are no longer with us.

HOW TO BUILD ALTERED WHEELBASE CARS

CHAPTER 3

Good ideas are where you find them. We borrowed the leaping goat from Billy Jacobs' *Kid Goat Hemi Dart*. While Jacobs used it in a much larger size aft of the doors, we scaled it down and applied it to the front fenders. Even though our Dart is powered by a 440, Bob further riffed with the design by adding the magical number 426—in red—to the goat's flanks.

With the driver's side finished, Bob turns his attention to the passenger side of the Dart, reusing the paper patterns to get identical results. Don't discard these paper patterns. Retain them so the graphics can be restored after a fender bender or other damage to the paint.

The passenger side takes shape. Bob spent a full day applying the graphics and frequently jumped from element to element to give the paint some needed drying time before adding a second color or other detail that might cause smudging.

108 HOW TO BUILD ALTERED WHEELBASE CARS

CHAPTER 4

FUNNY FAIRMONT CONSTRUCTION OVERVIEW

The Fairmont went from being a forgettable commuter to an unforgettable memory maker. The addition of a later-model overhead cam V-8 will complete the radical transformation, but you can see the potential in it with the chassis work complete. In a sea of similar street machines, this one definitely stands out from the crowd.

The *Wilshire Shaker* Nova and *Rampage* Dart offer tangible proof the Match Bash building style can deliver amazing results. But is the Match Bash altered wheelbase aesthetic strong enough to transcend the subject vehicle? Is Match Bash alone the point of the mission, or is the host vehicle the primary determiner of a successful outcome?

These questions are valid because the soaring cost and shrinking supply of solid Novas, Chevelles, GTOs, Tempests, 442s, Darts, Barracudas, Coronets, Belvederes, Falcons, Fairlanes, Comets, and Mustangs from the 1960s is a major obstacle to getting started. So what happens when you take a modern vehicle platform and give it the altered wheelbase treatment?

To find out, let's transform a 1981 Ford Fairmont from a humble low-line commuter car into a stellar Match Bash delight. Keep in mind this is a sedan model rather than the more flashy Futura Coupe. With its oddball delta-shaped B-pillar, the Futura is just too evocative of the Disco era and kills the Match Bash buzz. By contrast, the low-level sedan shares its boxy roof, vertical B-pillar, and less-is-more vibe with the 1960s factory-built Super Stockers we cherish today. Squint and you'll see it too.

When it was introduced for the 1978 model year, the Fox-platform Fairmont and its Mercury Zephyr cousin entered an automotive landscape that was reeling from the combined impacts of the OPEC energy crisis, federally mandated Corporate Average Fuel Economy (CAFE) standards, emission control devices, and a series of economic recessions.

Upon initial inspection, the Fairmont was a dog from a performance standpoint. Or was it? By comparison with the Maverick—which it replaced as Ford's low-price, mid-size offering—the Fairmont was a radical departure made possible by a vast influx of Ford executives with European experience. William O. Bourke, the ex-chairman of Ford of Europe was made executive vice president of North American Operations and Robert Alexander, who had served Ford of Europe as vice president in charge of its car-product development group, was brought to the States in the same capacity.

As a direct result, the Fairmont and Zephyr made a radical departure from Ford's big-car philosophy where excess mass was pawned off as "road-hugging weight" in company advertising. By contrast, the Fox platform cars were the most efficient Ford family sedans ever built, from a space-per-weight perspective. In the September 1977 issue of *Car and Driver*, Don Sherman writes, "Everywhere you look in the Fairmont, you see fat punched out with 'Swiss-cheesing' of internal body parts, cross-members and inner door panels. It may be smooth and planar on the outside, but it's riddled on the inside with weight-saving holes, just like a B-52."

So while the Fairmont never came factory equipped with anything hotter than a 302-ci 2-barrel, its light weight makes it a prime candidate for high-performance work. This point was demonstrated one year later when, in 1979, Ford introduced the new Mustang and Mercury Capri. Sharing the Fairmont's Fox platform—with the floorpan shortened 5.1 inches in front of the rear wheels and the cowl raised 1 inch (to allow a steeper hood slope angle for improved aerodynamics)—the Mustang, in 5.0-liter form, would rekindle the domestic rear-wheel-drive performance car market and single handedly ignite a new wave of Detroit horsepower engineering that hasn't let up since.

Amid the revived pony car wars, the Fairmont was largely overlooked and served yeoman duty shuffling satisfied families around the nation. The only performance highlights came in the form of the 2.3 turbo and ESO (European Sport Option) packages. There were no exciting GT or SVO performance derivatives for the Fairmont, a detail that has much to do with its general lack of desirability in gearhead circles today. The same guys who worship the ground beneath a 5.0 Mustang bash the Fairmont mercilessly. If those guys only knew…without the umbrella effect of the Fairmont's strong business case as a bread-and-butter family car, there would never have been a Mustang offshoot.

One notable Fairmont starburst was Bob Glidden's incredibly successful 1978 NHRA Pro Stock Futura. Built with assistance from Texas match race legend Don Hardy in just two weeks, Glidden's Fairmont made its debut on July 8, 1978, when it won the Edgewater Winston Championship Series (WCS) and set a national record of 8.76 seconds. Though it was retired at the end of the 1978 race season in favor of an equally successful Plymouth Arrow, the Cleveland-V-8-motivated Fairmont carried Glidden to an amazing 25 consecutive round wins. He won the NHRA Grandnational, U.S. Nationals, Fall Nationals, World Finals, and Beech Bend WCS races, all of which helped Glidden capture his third national championship title. If anybody remembers a drag race Fairmont today, it is this car.

Getting back to our altered wheelbase Fairmont project, we're going to bring Match Bash to the next level and show that wheelbase juggling can be applied to newer cars with respectable results. But remember, even the most freestyle Match Bash project must pivot around factory engineering and respect—not insult—the Super Stock and Factory Experimental legacy. And it all starts with a suitable engine, an engine that represents the factory's best and brightest period-correct hardware. Just as Mopar Match Bash cars should use nothing less than Max-Wedge or Hemi power and GM builds must employ division-specific big-blocks, traditional Ford projects toggle between pushrod and SOHC 427 FE power. Nothing else is correct. Or is it?

So rather than outfit the Match Bash Fairmont with a vintage FE powerplant or wimp out and settle for a small-block or boring 385-series (429, 460, 514) big-block, why not celebrate Ford's recent family of Cammer engines? It's a perfect match. Let's take today's best and brightest factory V-8, massage it for even more power, and stick it in a retro-themed late-model Fairmont.

FUNNY FAIRMONT CONSTRUCTION OVERVIEW

When Ford released a hotter 305-hp version of the DOHC for the 1996 SVT Cobra Mustang, Ford public relations circulated a great photo showing the new 4.6 mill flanked by a 427 SOHC and a Boss 429! External measurements of the trio are within a whisker and since then, Ford Racing Performance Parts (FRPP) and the performance aftermarket have really brought the DOHC 4.6 up to snuff. FRPP even markets a stroked 5.0-liter DOHC crate engine and calls it the Cammer, an age-old pet name for the 427 SOHC!

The altered wheelbase, pervasive retro cues, period-correct graphics, and massive Cammer should earn the car acceptance from even the most ardent Match Bash purist.

And truth be told, if I had an original 427 SOHC at my disposal, I wouldn't squander it on a project like this. I'd hunt down a 1966 Mustang 2+2 fastback and get going on a Holman-Moody stretch-nose replica. But since dollars don't fall from the sky, this "new car/new engine done retro" theme sets the pace.

Sure, there are plenty of expensive bits to obtain before any Match Bash project hits the street and strip, but the initial buy-in on a late-model project like this is a fraction of what it costs to get the ball rolling on a Match Bash tribute based on a more desirable 1960s vehicle. Think it over and watch as the *Funny Fairmont* gets funnied.

HOW TO BUILD ALTERED WHEELBASE CARS

CHAPTER 4

Plan and Prepare for Surgery

Though Bob Glidden dominated Pro Stock in a Fairmont Futura, the crazy delta-shaped B-pillar is a little over the top (literally) and clashes with the reserved austerity of a properly conceived Match Bash tribute car.

The basic Fairmont sedan is a much cleaner, no-frills design that's a direct descendent of 1960s strippers and Super Stocks. Notice that the sedan's taillight panel is not steeply angled like the Futura's.

With a mere 88 hp, the stock six-banger has got to go. But since this car lives in smog-conscious California where late-model engine swaps are closely regulated, we'll build the car around the six and swap it out later.

We spotted our sedan in the local classifieds and negotiated the seller down from $1,500 to $900. A rust-free California car, it's powered by the 3.3-liter (200-cube) six. Options include automatic transmission, air conditioning, power steering, bench seat, and AM/FM radio.

The massive 4-valve Ford 4.6 DOHC V-8 (left) Mod motor is slightly wider than a 426 Hemi. But with its all-aluminum construction, a complete engine weighs in at about 669 pounds. If the $14,995 price of a Ford Racing and Performance Parts (FRPP) crate Cammer (PN M6007-T50EA) isn't in your price range, rebuildable Lincoln MkVIII DOHC donor engines can commonly be found for under $500 at self-serve salvage yards. The only hassle is the Lincoln-specific siamesed-intake-port cylinder heads and induction. Mustang Cobra heads are preferred since they have non-siamesed single-intake runners and accept a wider range of induction systems.

FUNNY FAIRMONT CONSTRUCTION OVERVIEW

This mocked-up 4-valve Mod motor simulates the 8-stack Kinsler EFI system that transforms it into a worthy successor to the mighty Hilborn-injected 427 SOHC—a Ford match racing legend. The engine is the heart and soul of any Match Bash project and it needs to be right. Without the existence of the modern 4.6 DOHC engine, we wouldn't build this car. The Kinsler induction is not compatible with Lincoln Mk VIII heads and must be used with the less common Mustang Cobra-style heads. Coast High Performance and others sell remanufactured Mod motors and parts including 5.1-liter stroker kits.

Ford also builds 4.6 Mod motors with single overhead cams and 2-valve heads. Here's a wild 2-valve with a hand-built individual runner EFI system. Built by Ford Mod motor guru Richard Holdener, with that wild induction system, it's kinky enough for modern Match Bash use. The proper engine should capture the spirit of factory experimentation.

In the 1960s, a plastic dashboard assembly would have been reserved for the most exotic factory race cars. But it's standard equipment in every Fairmont (and Fox Mustang). Removing the padded vinyl dash cover allows access to the air-conditioning ducts and heater unit for removal. Less is more.

Even though it's made of lightweight plastic, removal of the in-car climate control components sheds an impressive 30 pounds.

Under the hood, eliminating the air-conditioning compressor, condenser, and hoses reduces another 70 pounds from the nose of the car.

The stock seats, headliner, carpet, and many pounds of sound-insulation padding are removed from the interior prior to surgery to prevent fire.

The wax-like seam sealer must be removed from all work areas since it can pollute the welds.

Fortunately, the seam sealer dissolves when sprayed with Gunk aerosol parts cleaner. With the metal and plastic body plugs removed from the interior and trunk floor, use a running hose to squirt the liquefied sealer out of the car. It's a messy, but necessary, job. Here's the same area of the rear wheel house after cleaning.

The stock trunk floor has a large spare tire well that's not necessary for Match Bash use. Drill through the spot welds and it drops free.

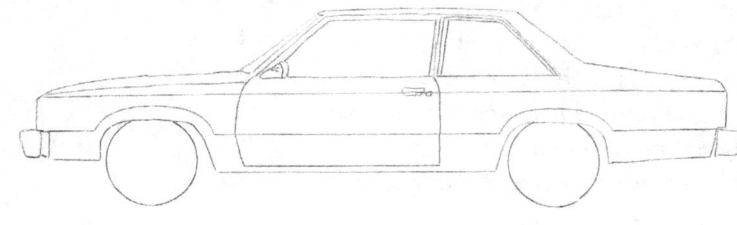
Before cutting, a tracing of the side profile drawing is taken from a photograph to assist in determining the aesthetic impact of wheel movement. Make several copies so you can try different treatments.

The metal well has many useful shapes that can be cut out and used for patches, so don't throw it away.

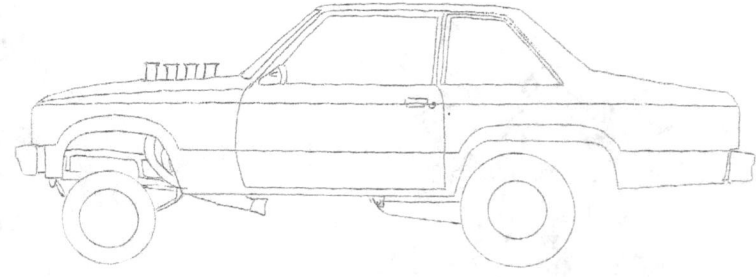
This drawing demonstrates the approximate impact of the chosen 11-inch rear wheel relocation. The front wheel opening has been moved forward in the fender—a painstaking and risky operation that requires advanced bodyworking skills for attractive results.

FUNNY FAIRMONT CONSTRUCTION OVERVIEW

Move the Rear Wheels

1. The areas to be manipulated must be carefully plotted on each side of the body. They are marked here with 1/4-inch pin striping tape. Using fixed reference points, such as the distance from door gaps, the window sills and other features common to both sides of the body ensure symmetry and eliminate distortion. On the Fairmont, there is a very useful trim screw hole positioned in the exact center of the wheel lip that is in perfect alignment with the axle centerline on both sides of the car.

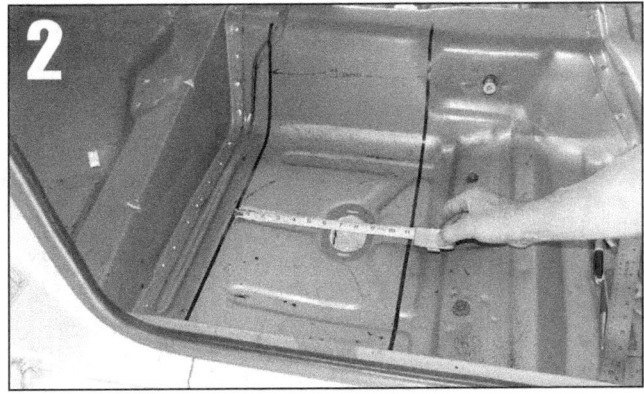

2. The same pin striping tape marks the 11-inch section of floor that must be removed to make way for the forward movement of the rear suspension module once it has been cut free from the rest of the car.

3. Once the internal and external cut lines are determined, the car must be evenly supported to prevent the body shell from flexing, sagging, or moving during surgery. Jack stands are positioned under the rear bumper, B-pillar, cowl, and front bumper.

4. Making sure the body remains level, the car must be lifted and supported by the frame so the rear suspension is unloaded and rear tires come into light contact with the ground. This is important, as the rear suspension module will ride on the tires as it rolls forward into its new position.

5. This view shows the quartet of floor jacks used to support the mid section of the body for surgery. Wood shims are placed between the frame and jacks to eliminate gaps so the body cannot rock as work is performed.

HOW TO BUILD ALTERED WHEELBASE CARS

CHAPTER 4

The front of the car must not be supported by the suspension because the springs will let the body bounce and could disrupt critical alignments. Supports placed beneath the rigidly mounted front bumper eliminate the threat.

Ace fabricator Dale Snoke pauses before making the first incision. He prefers to use a pneumatic cut-off wheel; a reciprocating saw can stub its long blade against hidden inner structures and flaw the integrity of the cuts.

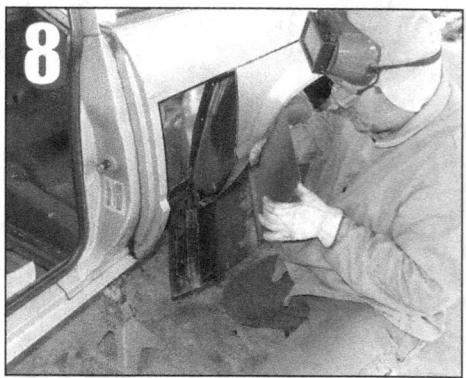

All incisions must be made as straight as possible to ease re-alignment. Don't discard the body skin; it will be reused as patch material.

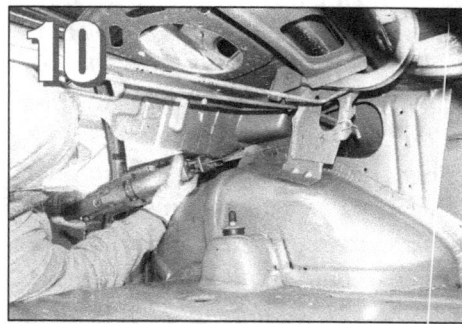

The separation of the suspension module from the body continues as Dale uses the reciprocating saw to detach the bracing between the wheel houses and the speaker shelf. These structures will be re-connected, so don't destroy them.

The trunk divider brace connects the speaker shelf to the suspension module and must be temporarily removed.

The rear passenger floorboards are removed with the plasma cutter, though the drive shaft tunnel remains to provide temporary strength while the separation work continues.

HOW TO BUILD ALTERED WHEELBASE CARS

FUNNY FAIRMONT CONSTRUCTION OVERVIEW

Here's the 11-inch gap left after body skin removal. Note that the stock shoulder-safety-belt anchor point remains attached to the B-pillar. We'll keep it until the roll bar and five-point driver safety harness are installed.

Here are the major sections of body skin and floor metal that are removed to allow the rear axle to move forward 11 inches.

The plasma cutter continues the task of separating the suspension module from the surrounding vehicle structure. The objective is to draw a perimeter around the suspension module and cut it free so it can be rolled forward. Here the trunk floor is sliced width-wise.

Rather than move the entire wheel house, Dale sliced it in a zig-zag pattern so the rear segment, quarter panel lip, trunk hinge supports, and related structures remain in their stock locations. The area to the left of the cut is part of the suspension module that is about to be rolled forward.

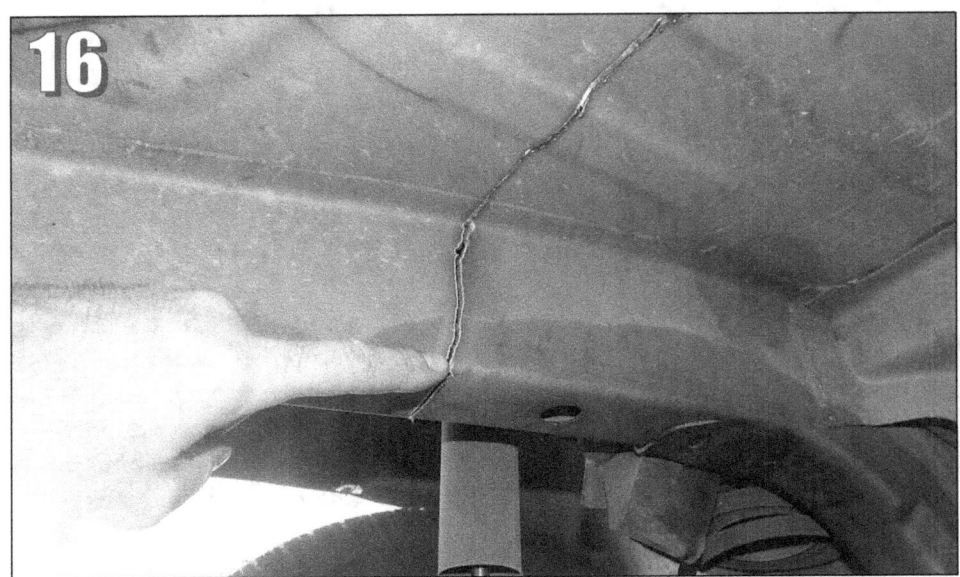

My finger points to more cut lines in the rear frame rails made with the plasma cutter. The rear perimeter of the suspension module is now fully separated from the body.

HOW TO BUILD ALTERED WHEELBASE CARS 119

This is the over-axle section of the floorpan. The tape measure indicates the 11-inch gap that will be filled once the suspension module is pushed forward on its wheels. But there is still more cutting to do.

Moving to the leading end of the suspension module, the boxed rocker sills are sliced open with the plasma cutter.

A claw hammer separates metal after slicing.

Removing the inner wall of the rocker sills makes clearance for the suspension module to move forward and dock.

Up to this point, the center portion of the driveshaft tunnel has been retained to maintain support during cutting. Now it is removed and replaced by a jack stand to prevent unwanted motion. The car is very delicate at this stage so be careful not to stomp around during surgery.

With the entire inner perimeter of the suspension module separated from the body, the final cuts are made to the external quarter panels to free the module for relocation.

FUNNY FAIRMONT CONSTRUCTION OVERVIEW

Before movement, the markings show the stock alignment of the C-pillars.

These markings show the stock alignment of the rocker sill boxes.

The arrows indicate the stock alignment of the trunk hump prior to alteration.

Here's a final look at the severed wheel house. Soon, all of the markings shown in the preceding photos will be separated by an 11-inch gap.

With all connections severed and interfering panels cut away, the suspension module is slowly rolled forward beneath the supported body into its new position, 11 inches closer to the front axle centerline.

HOW TO BUILD ALTERED WHEELBASE CARS

CHAPTER 4

The docked suspension module offers a first glimpse at the world's only altered wheelbase Match Bash Fairmont. The wheelbase just shrank from 105½ to 94½ inches, approximately reversing the front/rear static weight bias from 52/48 to 48/52.

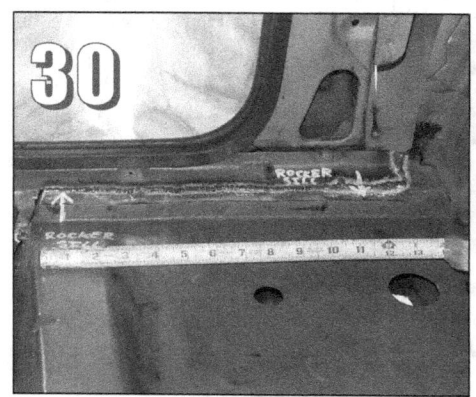

The 11-inch realignment of the arrows is mute testimony to the wheelbase alteration process.

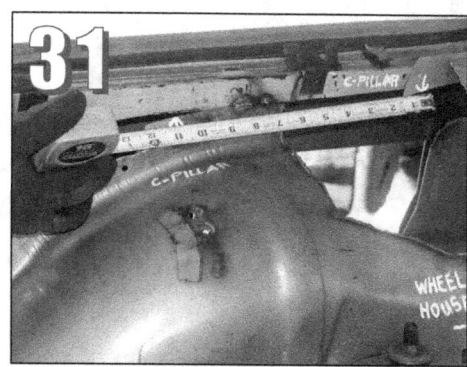

This is the C-pillar area after the 11-inch wheelbase shift. Again, by keeping the entire suspension module as a one-piece unit, the job is greatly simplified.

After the move, notice the 11-inch span between the sections of the rear wheel house. This is the passenger side.

A floor jack is placed beneath the leading end of the loose suspension module to close the panel gaps prior to welding. The initial care taken to support the body so the rear tires are in very light floor contact neutralizes any tendency for the rear coil springs to push the module up and cause misalignment problems.

After precisely adjusting the suspension module to equalize the wheelbase from side to side, reattachment begins. The first union consists of a series of spot welds along the quarter panel seam. Full welding of the seams will be done later, after the frame and inner structure connections are restored.

FUNNY FAIRMONT CONSTRUCTION OVERVIEW

The driver-side quarter panel is rejoined with the body. Low-heat spot welds minimize distortion and reduce the amount of bodywork required.

Reattachment continues as the suspension module is welded to the rocker sills.

The floor and drive shaft tunnel are welded back together. It all looks nearly stock, except for the fact rear-seat passengers no longer have a place to put their feet. The rear seat has been eliminated.

Segments of 2½-inch, 1/8-inch-thick rectangular steel tubing fit inside the stock factory frame rails and are welded in place. This reconnects the suspension module to the rear of the frame.

A second layer of frame—made from a sliced portion of rectangular tubing—is welded atop the main segment to build height so it matches the level of the trunk floor.

HOW TO BUILD ALTERED WHEELBASE CARS

CHAPTER 4

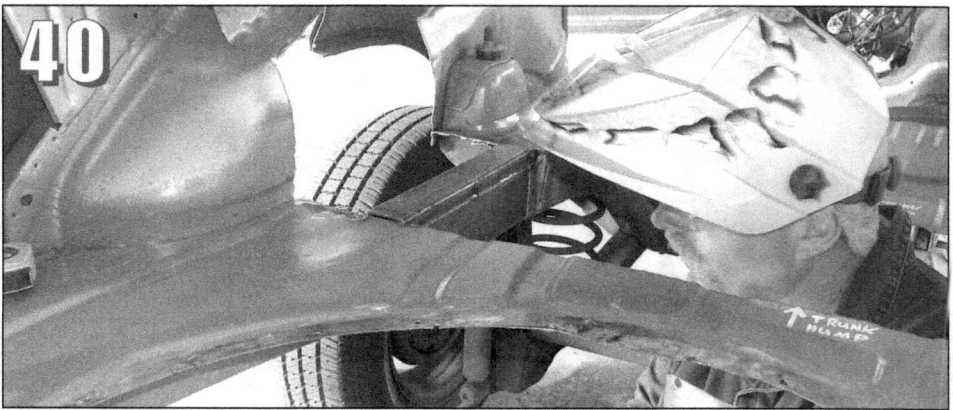

With the suspension module re-welded to the body, strength is fully restored. Now the rear tires can be removed and the car supported by the rear axle so patching of the wheel house and trunk floor can begin.

The many post-surgery gaps are easily covered with sheet steel.

Using patch material that's the same thickness as the parent material makes welding easier, since the molten welding wire bonds to the old and new panels at the same rate. A Plymouth Duster hood skin shares its .050-inch thickness with the Fairmont's inner structures.

The gap over the rear axle is filled with Duster hood metal after careful trimming and contouring.

More loose scraps are trimmed and hammered in place to serve as wheel house filler patches. This is the view from the driver side of the trunk.

The passenger-side wheel house is patched in similar fashion. If you think this work is too crude, check out period photos of vintage match racers and you'll see similar techniques. This is how they were done. Fully welded seams will keep tire smoke out of the cabin.

FUNNY FAIRMONT CONSTRUCTION OVERVIEW

The hole left by the spare tire tub must be patched. The inverted tub is used as a template to mark an outline on a sheet of .050-inch steel. The plasma cutter makes quick work of the cut, though a jig saw will also suffice.

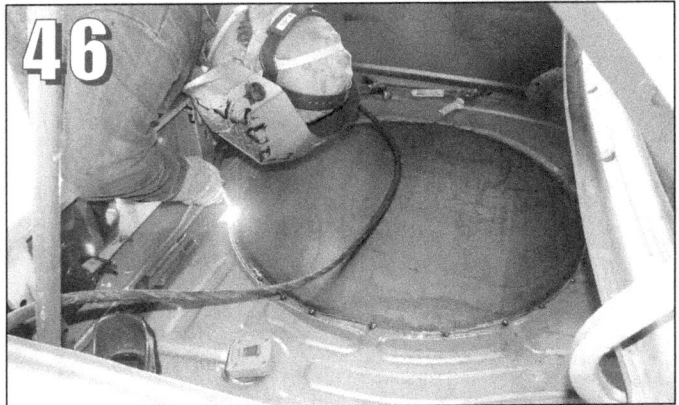

The patch is welded in place. A sanitary trunk compartment is desirable in any Match Bash car since it'll showcase the trunk-mounted Mopar Super Stock battery—a classic match race trick for extra ballast over the slicks.

The final step involves making patches to fill the gaps in the wheel openings. Rather than attempt to form the required complex curves in one piece of metal, Dale simplifies the job by using several small pieces.

The patches are cut so they merge on existing body lines to reduce the amount of finish bodywork required.

The passenger-side fender lip is entirely hand formed. Small tack welds hold everything in place.

HOW TO BUILD ALTERED WHEELBASE CARS

CHAPTER 4

All seams are fully welded for maximum strength. Dale welds the thin-gauge body skin in small sections and frequently jumps from one spot to another. This minimizes localized heating and reduces panel distortion.

With the welds ground smooth, ace body man Mike Morgan applies plastic body filler to hide the scars.

By working carefully to maintain surface height during the patching operation, only a thin coat of body filler is needed for smooth results.

The final step is re-welding the trunk divider brace back into position. This important stamping ties the wheel houses and C-pillars into the floor for rigidity and should not be omitted.

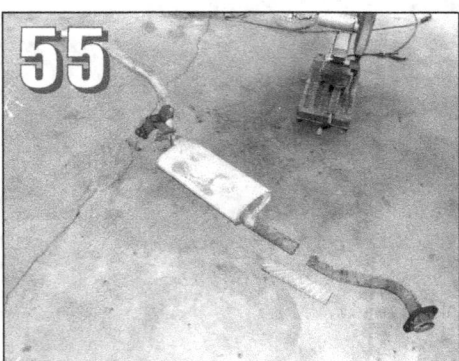

Dale celebrates a job well done. He accomplished the entire rear axle alteration job in a mere 27 hours. The stretched wheel opening mimics the effect used on Dyno Don Nicholson's 1965 SOHC Cyclone match racer.

Eleven inches are removed from the stock single-exhaust system so it can be retained after surgery. The leading end bolts to the catalytic converter for smog-compliant status.

FUNNY FAIRMONT CONSTRUCTION OVERVIEW

The driveshaft must also be shortened 11 inches to suit the reduced wheelbase.

Fairmonts and Mustangs share this highly effective four-link coil spring rear suspension design. With minimal upgrades (tubular control arms and heavy duty shocks) it'll put any Fox into the 10-second zone with slicks. The stock Fairmont rear axle has a 7½-inch ring gear and is not strong enough for high-performance use. This axle was installed in pre-1986 5.0 Mustangs and is a weak link. The four-lug axles severely limit wheel selection.

In 1986 Ford introduced the rugged 8.8-inch rear axle for use in 5.0 Mustang applications. It is a direct swap into the Fairmont and can handle 400 hp in stock form. Swapping the stock four-lug axle shafts with two driver-side axles and brake drums from any Ford Bronco II or Ranger pickup allows the use of five-lug wheels. The truck-sourced brake drums are 9 inches in diameter and are compatible with the stock Fairmont brake assembly. The Fairmont station wagon coil springs use .6-inch-diameter wire (.05 thicker than a 2-door sedan) and add 1 inch of ride height.

A quick coat of primer protects the bodywork. The junkyard axle swap delivers a 5-on-4½-inch bolt circle, allowing installation of 15 x 7-inch Chrysler steel wheels and beefy rear tires. The semi-finished altered wheelbase job transforms the car, but we're not done!

HOW TO BUILD ALTERED WHEELBASE CARS

CHAPTER 4

"Swiss Cheese" the Rear Bumper

Six bolts secure the rear bumper. There is an unsightly steel reinforcement riveted to the backside of the bumper. As shown, the unit weighs 25 pounds.

Grinding the rivet heads frees the brace for removal. Removal is not driven by the quest for weight savings. Rather, this ugly brace will be visible through the holes we're about to cut unless it is eliminated.

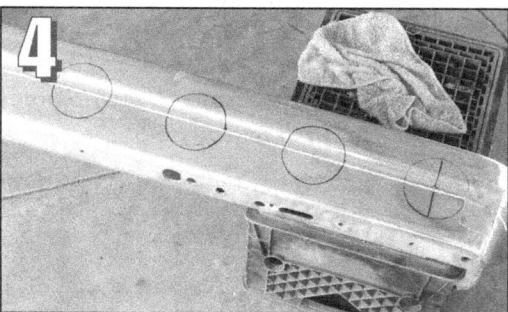

Light aluminum bumpers were featured on legendary factory Super Stockers like the 1962–1963 Pontiac Super Duty, 1964 Ford Thunderbolt, 1963 and 1964 Mopar Max-Wedge and 1964 Race Hemi, and 1963 Chevy Z-11 Impala. In the post-OPEC era, aluminum bumpers were embraced to boost fuel economy and the Fairmont is no exception. Its aluminum 5-mph bumpers may not be graceful but they're in keeping with the Match Bash mood. Let's take it even further with the hole saw.

Eight 3½-inch holes are marked on the bumper with a felt-tip pen. Be sure to double-check their location for symmetry and even alignment for attractive results.

A 3½-inch hole saw makes quick work of the soft aluminum. The central pilot hole maintains alignment.

The modified bumper weighs 18 pounds, delivering a 7-pound weight reduction and a major boost in Match Bash appeal.

FUNNY FAIRMONT CONSTRUCTION OVERVIEW

Install Straight Front Axle

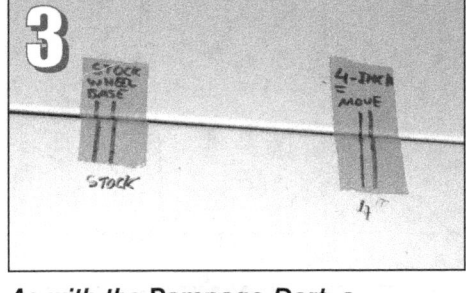

The Fairmont's simple body lines welcome fender surgery to shift the front wheel openings forward. Just remove the vertical rectangles ahead of the wheels, slice the fender openings free, and slide them forward. The same welding and patching technique used at the rear wheels openings finishes the job. It's a valid Match Bash strategy, but in the end it was decided to simply trim the offending metal for tire clearance.

Fairmont chassis engineers reinterpreted the MacPherson strut design by positioning the coil spring inboard, between the frame and lower control arm, instead of around the strut. Watch those coil springs during disassembly. They retain plenty of stored energy even when unloaded. Use a spring compressor for safe removal.

As with the Rampage Dart, a weighted string is affixed to the hood and draped over the fender so it aligns with the stock wheel spindle centerline. The mark is transferred onto the hood, along with another mark depicting the desired 4-inch axle relocation. By moving the string forward and re-affixing it on the new mark, the hanging string can be used to accurately establish the new front spindle centerline. The hood should not be removed during surgery or these critical reference points can be disturbed.

Just as with the rear suspension surgery, the entire car is supported on jack stands so it is perfectly level with the ground. We'll leave the stock engine in position during the frame fabrication to avoid ugly surprises later on. We start by removing the front sheetmetal for easy access but leave the hood in place. The new axle centerline marks will guide front axle installation.

Three bolts secure the tops of the struts and a spring compressor is used to remove the coil spring.

HOW TO BUILD ALTERED WHEELBASE CARS

CHAPTER 4

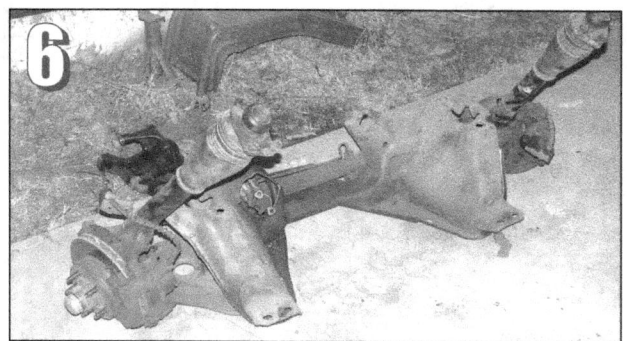

Thanks to the separate K-frame design, the entire front suspension unit drops out once the steering coupler, top shock mounts, and four frame-attachment bolts are removed. At nearly 200 pounds, this stuff is headed for the scrap bin.

Since the motor mounts are removed with the K-frame, a jack stand placed beneath the harmonic balancer supports the front of the engine while the transmission mount supports the rear. A bubble balance placed atop the air cleaner ensures stock engine positioning for carburetor float function and driveshaft angle.

With the fenders temporarily reinstalled, baseline measurements are taken by propping a loose wheel in the stock location. The weighted string is aligned with the stock spindle location in this photo. To maintain a graceful balance, front axle relocation should never be more than half the distance the rear axle is moved. The greater functional and aesthetic impact of wheelbase manipulation is delivered at the rear of the car. The front axle relocation is a secondary effect that must not overshadow the work done at the rear.

The weighted string confirms the 11-inch rear axle relocation is nicely complimented by a 4-inch move at the front. The effect is subtle yet shocking.

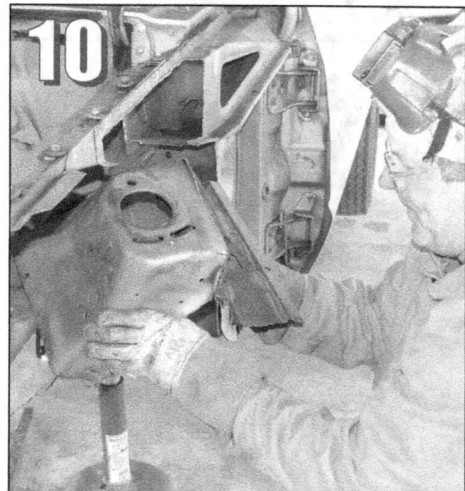

Dale starts by removing all traces of the stock fender aprons and strut towers using the plasma cutter. The upper fender-mounting shelf remains undisturbed so the fenders can be accurately positioned during reassembly. Holman-Moody employed a similar strategy on the 1965 and 1966 SOHC Mustangs.

FUNNY FAIRMONT CONSTRUCTION OVERVIEW

Here's the scene after the unnecessary sheetmetal is removed. To a lazy builder, the lower frame rail extensions may look like a tempting place to mount the leaf spring brackets. But measurements reveal it is located too high above the ground and would require either absurdly arched leaf springs or impractically long mounting stanchions to deliver the desired nose-up ride height. The stock frame rail extensions must go.

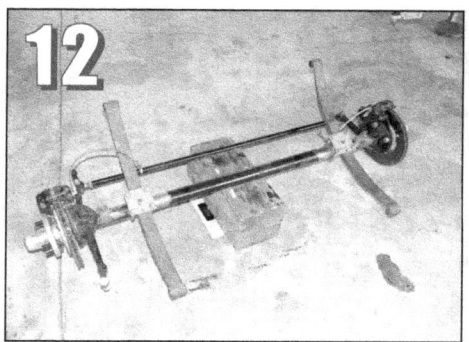

Our reinforced Specialty Cars straight axle weighs 67 pounds, the springs weigh 9½ pounds each, and the Wilwood vented disc brake kit (PN 140-2260) weighs 28 pounds for a total of 114 pounds. It is important to hit the correct axle width to avoid an unsightly too-wide or too-narrow front track measurement. This one is 56½ inches wide (48 inches kingpin-to-kingpin) and gives the Fairmont a just-right, sure-footed stance. When in doubt, duplicating the stock front track measurement is a safe bet. Loaded, the height distance between the spring eyes and spindle nut is 5½ inches. Do not weld the spring pads to the axle tube until after final width and caster requirements are determined.

The ideal Match Bash stance places the front axle spindle nut approximately level with the bottom of the rocker panel (when viewed from the side). To achieve this, the new lower frame rail location is carefully considered. The 5½-inch arch of the loaded leaf springs dictates the horizontal position of the new frame rails. Here Dale test fits a section of 2 x 3-inch square tubing prior to welding it to the firewall and radiator bulkhead. Copious test fitting and bubble-level checking is vital to ensure that the frame rails are parallel front-to-rear and also perfectly horizontal to the ground. Any deviations will result in a crooked race car. The Fairmont's frame rails are spaced exactly 30¼ inches apart.

After welding in the new frame rail just below the original, the reciprocating saw is used to remove the stock frame rail extension from the body. The frame replacement work is done on one side of the car at a time to avoid the potential for sagging and shifting.

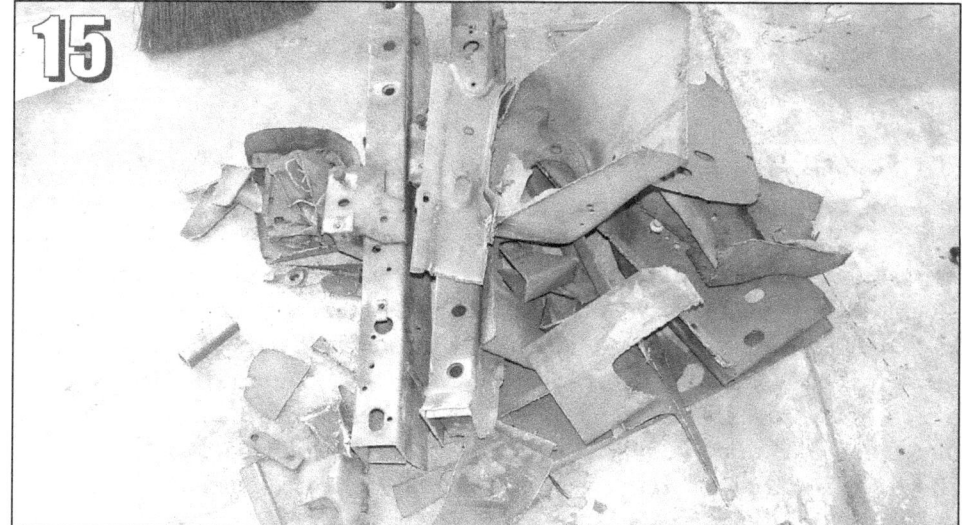

Here are the stock frame extensions, shock towers, and inner fender material trimmings just before they go in the trash.

HOW TO BUILD ALTERED WHEELBASE CARS

CHAPTER 4

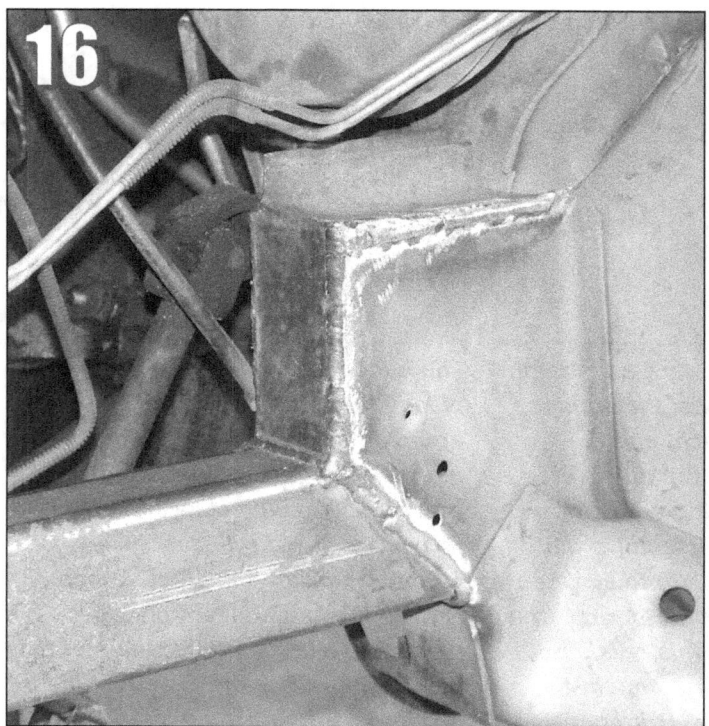

After they are capped with welded steel plate, the stock frame extension stumps make an excellent hard-point upon which to mount the new 2 x 3-inch frame rails. This is the driver's side after welding.

Ford designed extra strength into the upper cowl area to absorb crash forces. We take advantage of these rugged box-like structures by cutting them flush and welding on steel plates. The caps serve as hard-points for mounting of the diagonal upper frame braces.

The diagonal upper frame braces are made of 1.650-inch steel tubing and bolster the lower frame rails against bending loads. For simplicity, the stock radiator bulkhead and hood latch mechanism are retained at this point, though classic hood pins will appear in the future. Thick steel plates are welded to the bulkhead and the tubes are welded to the plates. This spreads the load into a stronger surface than the thin-gauge factory radiator bulkhead stamping.

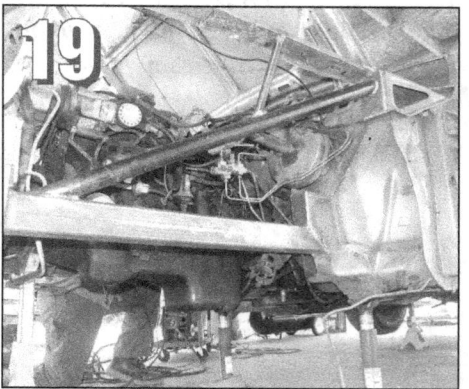

Here's a look at the completed frame structure on the driver's side. Tough as a tank, it's far stronger than the factory design and is a close copy of designs used on wheel-standing 1960s-era exhibition cars. Note that a single 7/8-inch tubular strut has been welded between the diagonal brace and the fender-mounting shelf for added rigidity.

Dale fabricated a pair of motor-mount outriggers to support the six-cylinder engine using the stock rubber motor-mount isolators. Once the Cammer is ready, these mounts will be removed and reworked to suit the different location of the V-8 motor-mount bosses.

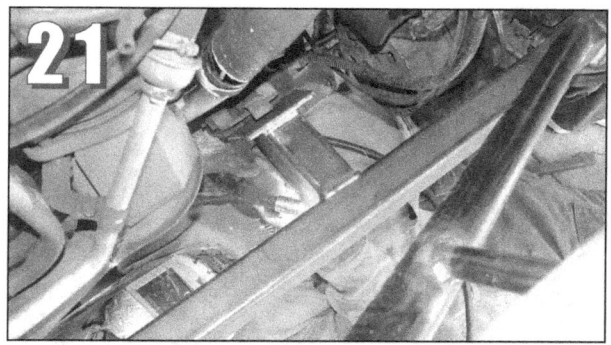

Welded to the frame, the new motor mounts allow removal of the jack stand supporting the engine so work can begin on the leaf spring mounts.

Dale makes the rear leaf spring mounts from sections of 2½ x 2½-inch square tubing with one wall trimmed off to yield the U-section. They are drilled with 1/2-inch holes to accept Grade 8 spring eye bolts.

With the amount of front axle centerline manipulation established at 4 inches ahead of stock, the rear spring mounts are welded to the frame rails with frequent measurements taken to ensure symmetry from side to side. The leaf springs are 1¾ inches wide, but the eye bushings are wider and fit perfectly inside the new mounts.

We mount the articulated spring shackles to the forward ends of the leaf springs. To accept them, we use Specialty Cars trick tubular upper shackle hangars. Made of 1/4-inch-thick, 1⅜-inch steel tubing, these hangars can be welded to virtually any flat surface and are much easier to install than more complicated gusseted-plate-type hangars. Dale placed a fat bead of weld all around them for maximum strength. After the leaf springs are mounted to the car, install the axle using the U-bolts and plates from the kit and center it precisely. Then, tip it so there is between 6 and 8 degrees of positive caster (the bottom of the king pin leading the top) and weld the spring pads to the axle tube once and for all.

Before we discuss the cardboard template, note that the spring shackle is leaning 20 degrees from vertical with the lower pivot point ahead of the upper pivot point. This is the ideal orientation for proper suspension function and prevents spring bind on compression. Before the upper hangar is welded to the frame the spring must be loaded with full vehicle weight and the desired 20-degree shackle angle must be established. Getting back to the cardboard template, it's an aid in fabricating the steering box mount.

The template outline is transferred onto a plate of 3/8-inch steel with chalk.

The plasma cutter neatly trims the mount from the steel.

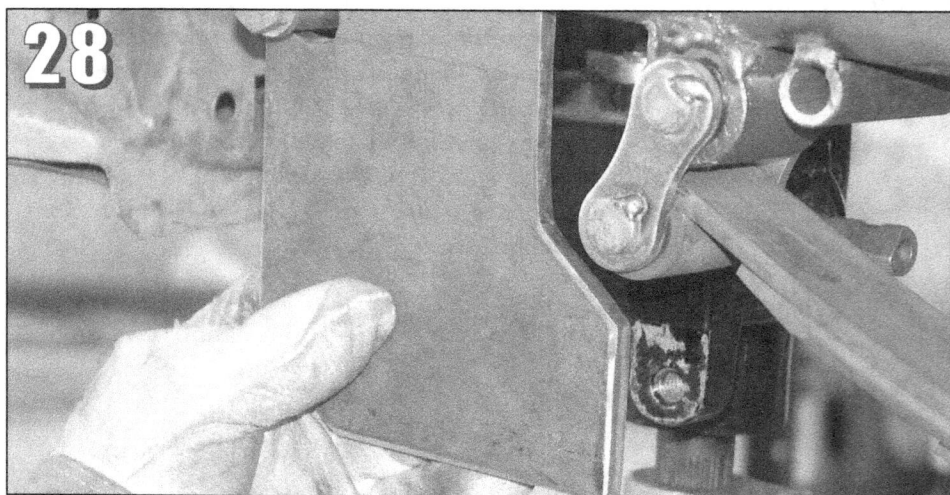

Prior to welding, the steering box mount is clamped in position to determine if final adjustment is needed. The objective is to position the steering box in direct alignment with the steering column and wheel. A straight shot is best for simplicity. At the same time, the pitman arm must be parallel with the ground for proper linkage geometry.

After welding and the addition of welded tubular spacers, the Flaming River steering box is bolted to the mount using Grade 8 fasteners. This is a view from below.

Viewed from above, the trio of tubular steel spacers is visible. Also in view is the Flaming River U-joint that mates the steering box to the Flaming River 3/4-inch steering column tube.

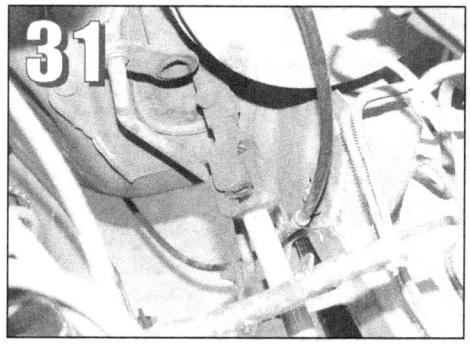

The stock Fairmont steering shaft incorporates a Borgeson joint. A fully welded tubular union merges the stock shaft to the Flaming River extension.

Going back under the car, my finger points to a small clearance tunnel cut into the driverside motor-mount support to allow steering shaft passage. The tunneled section is re-boxed for maximum strength.

A single 3/4-inch spherical rod end welded to the frame rail supports the steering shaft between the two U-joints that connect it to the steering box and stock Fairmont steering column.

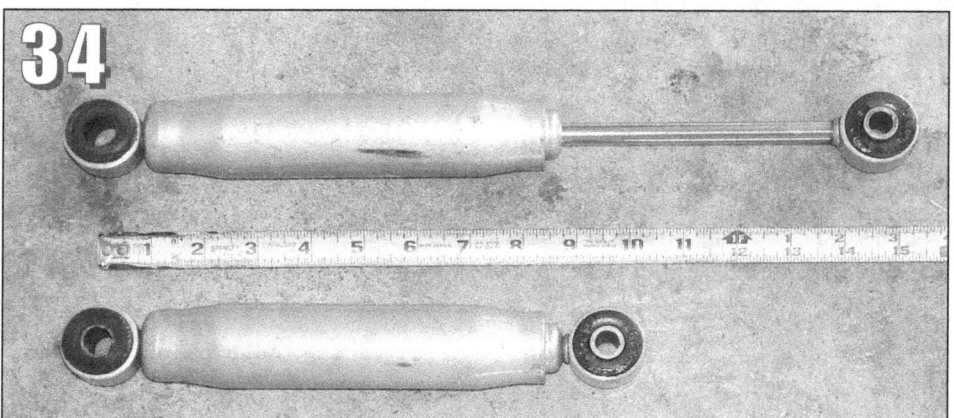

Most over-the-counter shock absorbers are too long for typical straight-axle installations, so Specialty Cars supplies these compact dampers. They measure $9\frac{1}{2}$ inches compressed and $14\frac{1}{2}$ inches extended and have 5 inches of travel.

Dale uses the plasma cutter to sculpt a set of shock absorber mounts out of 2 x 2-inch square tubing.

Prior to welding, set the shock mounts so the shock absorbers are in the middle of their travel range with the full weight of the car on the springs. A bubble level is used to equalize shock angles on both sides of the car while mounts are welded to ensure equal roll-center behavior.

CHAPTER 4

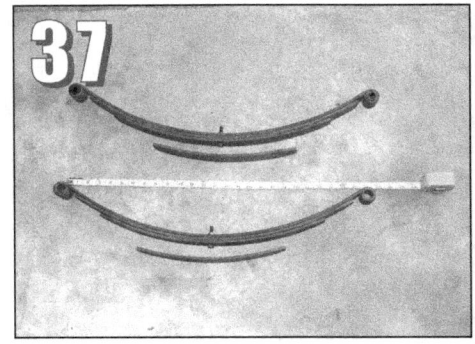

The four-leaf, 26-inch springs deliver a harsh ride with the light six-cylinder engine. When the heavier Cammer goes in, there will be more mass on the springs and the ride should improve. Removing the bottom leaf improved the ride with an acceptable 1/2-inch loss in ride height. If we do it over, we'll probably specify longer leaf springs like the ones used on the Wilshire Shaker *Nova*. The **Shaker's** four-leaf springs have the same 6-inch arch measurement, but at 34 inches center-to-center they provide a much smoother ride with no ride height penalty.

The straight-axle installation allows the complete removal of the stock strut towers from the engine bay. The wide Cammer won't fit otherwise.

Here is a view of the finished front suspension as viewed from the driver's side. With the weight removed from the suspension, notice how the unloaded spring becomes shorter and the shackle angle relaxes to a vertical orientation. This is why it is critically important to weld the upper shackle mount to the frame only when there is full vehicle weight on the springs.

The same view from the passenger side reveals the drag link (ahead of the axle tube) that receives steering box inputs and feeds them to the tie rod (behind the axle tube). This cross-steering arrangement is preferred over the near-steer strategy (where the steering box is coupled to the driver-side axle spindle). The long drag link mutes the effect of road shocks and body rise on the steering wheel for better driver control.

Steering articulation is firm and tight thanks to the new parts used throughout. Front shackle length should only be used to fine-tune ride height, never to establish it. Short shackles work best. Long shackles (more than 3 inches) can't resist lateral side loads and tend to lay-over, resulting in sloppy cornering traits. The shackles supplied in the Specialty Cars axle kit measure 1½ inches.

The braided-steel flexible brake hoses use compression fittings and 90-degree AN fittings to merge the stock Ford brake lines to the Wilwood calipers. We got them from G&J Aircraft in Ontario, California, for under $50 with all fittings included.

FUNNY FAIRMONT CONSTRUCTION OVERVIEW

After all fabrication is complete, the front clip is stripped and a coat of Rust-Oleum Smoke Gray brush paint is applied to the raw metal.

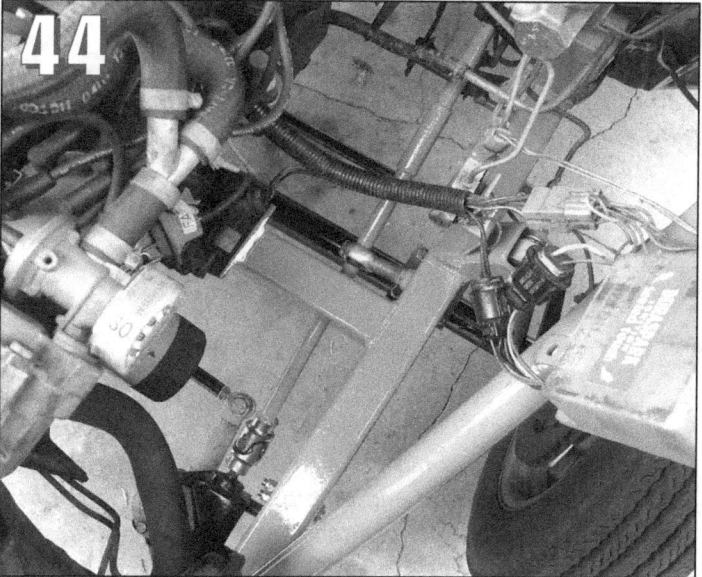

After a week of drying time the front suspension is reinstalled. Here's a final look at the steering column and driverside motor mount. Note that all stock underhood equipment (Duraspark ignition module, evaporative emissions charcoal canister, inlet air supply tube, etc.) are mounted in their original locations via temporary supports and metal tabs. California cars built after 1974 must pass a visual test during bi-annual smog inspections. These underhood items must not be disturbed.

The increased ride height provides plenty of clearance for the Coker reproduction BF Goodrich 6.00-15-inch front tires without fender trimming. Cragar S/S wheels are a perfect choice and were very popular on many vintage match racers. Note that finish bodywork has not been performed on the driver's side of the body. A heavy coat of clear urethane protects the exposed metal.

The proper engine for this job is a Ford Racing and Performance Parts 2003–2004 Mustang Mach 1 crate engine (PN M-6007-M146, $5,700). Rated at 305 hp, it's a virtual clone to the naturally aspirated engines used in the 1999–2002 Mustang SVT Cobra. The exception is the way the Mach 1 was factory fitted with a Shaker hood scoop and camshafts borrowed from the Lincoln 5.4 InTech SUV mill for extra mid-range torque. In six-cylinder mode, the Funny Fairmont weighed 2,520 pounds with a full tank of gas.

HOW TO BUILD ALTERED WHEELBASE CARS

CHAPTER 4

Initially altered in California, the Fairmont's 200-cube six-popper had to stay put in order to pass the Golden State's bi-annual visual and tailpipe emissions tests. But after a move to Massachusetts in 2008 (car and author)—where smog laws are more realistic—the 4.6 engine swap became a valid option. The sleepy six-banger and C4 automatic were listed on eBay Motors where they sold for $1.25 in a no-reserve sale. I made the buyer pay me in pennies so I'd feel like I actually got something substantial for it. And no, I didn't discover a 1909-S VDB wheat penny in the payment. The Tremec TKO-600 (PN M-7003-R58H, $1,850) and cast-aluminum bellhousing (PN M-6392-M46, $375) will replace the lame C4 automatic.

The wheel opening panel was moved forward in 1-inch increments to view the aesthetic effect of each shift. The most dynamic effect is achieved when the tire is positioned noticeably ahead of the centerline of the wheel opening, as if the chassis is trying to leap out from under the body shell. A 4-inch move was perfect for the job. Re-joining the wheel openings to the fender skins takes plenty of time so the welding heat doesn't become localized and cause warping. The fender metal removed allowed the wheel opening to be moved forward to fill the gaps created by the shift. Just juggle the metal patches so the contours are aligned. Minimal plastic body filler will cover the scars later. After axle surgery, the wheelbase grew from 98.5 to 102.5 inches. The stock wheelbase was 105.5 inches.

The nearly completed headers use 1⅝ primary tubes to suit the modest 281-inch displacement. Though zero "science" went into figuring primary tube length, the engine runs fine with none of the voodoo problems a few self-proclaimed experts predicted (over-scavenging, torque pulses, sonic booms, bad interplanetary karma, barking chickens, etc.). The black cam covers shown here were later replaced by 1996 Cobra covers, which have less "busy" surface features and more closely capture the feel of the 427 SOHC. The cost of header tubing materials was just under $422. Farming the job out to a custom header shop would easily cost four times as much.

As of this writing (July 2012), the Fairmont has been running with DOHC V-8 power for about eight weeks in the configuration shown here. With its previous 200-cube, six-cylinder engine it weighed exactly 2,520 pounds with a full tank of gas. Once the novelty of the altered wheelbase wore off, it was boring to drive. But now with its estimated 350 hp, approximate 2,700-pound curb weight (no dyno or scale session yet), 3.73:1 axle ratio, and 5-speed stick, it's a fun little screamer that gets many looks.

From a standing start and during violent power shifts, there's a tendency toward axle hop—a surprising trait given the Southside bars. But I attribute that to the worn-out shocks and spindly Fairmont V-8 station wagon coil springs I installed to get more rear tire clearance. Still, I'm seriously considering converting the rear suspension to Chrysler S/S leaf springs and a suitably narrowed Ford 9-inch this coming winter.

CHAPTER 5

MATCH BASH: OTHER VOICES

Even though drag racers stopped building altered wheelbase door-slammer match race cars soon after the 1966 arrival of the Mercury flip-top Comet funny cars, the modern Match Bash movement has fostered the construction of many altered wheelbase tribute cars and restorations of actual vintage warriors. Here's a selection from all over the country.

Richard "Mr. Rich" LeFebvre has been building Match Bash cars for nearly a decade. The Seattle-based entrepreneur has a keen eye for authenticity and works hard to get all the details right. His Gold Rush 1965 Coronet packs a Hilborn-injected Hemi, 727 Torqueflite, and lettering by Bob Thompson. This car was a four-door sedan before Rich's conversion.

HOW TO BUILD ALTERED WHEELBASE CARS   139

The Performance King 1965 Plymouth is another Hemi-powered Mr. Rich creation. Also lettered by Bob Thompson, the front wheels are rare magnesium American Racing Torq-Thrusts. Fully street legal, this Torqueflite-equipped barn stormer runs high 10s at the strip.

Recently completed, Rich isn't sure if he's going to have this sleek black 1965 Plymouth lettered or not. The Hilborn-injected Hemi sits atop a narrowed Dodge A100 van straight-axle shod with another set of rare magnesium Torq-Thrusts.

Augie Delgado of Los Angeles, California, resurrected this original L79 4-speed 1966 Nova from near death. Built for drag racing back in the 1960s, the original builders moved the rear axle forward 8 inches and installed a straight front axle. Word is, a supercharged Rat once powered it, but today Augie runs a Jackson-injected small-block coupled to a 4-speed stick.

MATCH BASH: OTHER VOICES

As found in 1998, the Nova was sitting in a storage lot and was about to be junked. The rear suspension consists of a Ford 9-inch with Thunderbolt-style traction arms, which Augie retained. He was even able to save the original radio delete plate.

Legendary match racer and header king Doug Thorley even got into the Match Bash game. Here's his recreation of the Chevy 2 Much Nova he campaigned back in the 1960s. It packs an injected Rat and is a dead ringer for the original car. Doug did most of the construction work himself.

Noted California Mopar collector Bob Munoa built the Injuneered 1965 Plymouth on his Indian reservation. The Race Hemi hood scoop is cut to clear the Hemi's Hilborn fuel injection stacks. A life-long Los Angeles firefighter, Bob painted it fire engine red.

HOW TO BUILD ALTERED WHEELBASE CARS

CHAPTER 5

Not a modern re-creation, this one is the real deal and shows there's plenty of interest in finding and restoring the few match racers that managed to survive. The Strip Teaser II Falcon was originally built in 1965 by Georgians Bob Thomas and Howard Neal with tuning by Larry Davis. It was a major player on the southern match race circuit and is now owned by Greg Sullivan, a Huntsville, Alabama, drag racing collector, and enthusiast.

The Strip Teaser II runs a 427 High-Riser wedge that originally powered Bob Thomas' 1964 Fairlane Thunderbolt. Larry Davis helped fabricate the unique, individual-runner mechanical fuel-injection unit—the first of its type to be installed on a Ford 427 wedge.

Seattle, Washington, landscaper Arnie Gundersen built this 1965 Plymouth Match Bash champ. With a Hilborn-injected Hemi, magnesium Torq-Thrusts and miniature Moon tank, Arnie captured the essence of the 1965 Mopar factory A/FX team right down to the relocated torsion bar front suspension. The Untoucha Bel II moniker is a brilliant example of how to pick a nostalgic-yet-original name for your Match Bash project.

Though outnumbered by Chevrolet, Ford, and Mopar competition, plenty of Pontiac, Buick, and Oldsmobile match racers were active back in the day. This in-process restoration of the original Lutz and Lundberg 1966 Olds 442 match racer is being performed by Jerry Chapman and Curt Anderson of Minnesota. Power comes from a supercharged 482-ci Olds. Though it'll likely be a strip-only machine once completed, there's no reason you can't build a streetable Match Bash 442 of your own.

Connecticut funny car fanatics Gary Gerard and Bill Atwood collaborated on the Flashback 1965 Plymouth Belvedere. Motivated by a cross-ram-equipped Race Hemi, full-manual 727 Torqueflite, and Dana 60 rear axle, it runs low 11s yet is regularly driven on the street in true Match Bash spirit.

SOURCE GUIDE

Appletree Automotive
1920 N. 24th Avenue
Mears, MI 49436
800-433-2521
www.appletreeauto.com
(Dart bucket seats)

AVH Technology
10942 Elliott Avenue
El Monte, CA 91733-2308
626-442-9291
avhlaser@aol.com

B&M Racing & Performance
9142 Independence Avenue
Chatsworth, CA 91311
818-882-6422
www.bmracing.com

Classic Industries
18460 Gothard Street
Huntington Beach, CA 92648
800-854-1280 Ext. 5210
www.classicindustries.com

Capana Speed & Performance
(Wilcap)
P.O. Box 14232
San Luis Obispo, CA 93406
805-481-7639
www.wilcap.com

Coast High Performance
2555 West 237th Street
Torrance, CA 90505
310-784-1010
www.coasthigh.com

Competition Engineering
80 Carter Drive
Guilford, CT 06437
203-453-5200
www.competitionengineering.com

Cragar Industries, Inc.
P.O. Box 558
Milford, IA 51351
877-827-2427
www.cragar.com

Currie Enterprises, Inc.
1480 N. Tustin Avenue
Anaheim, CA 92807
714-528-6957
www.currieenterprises.com

DynoWorks
346 S. I Street, Unit 8
San Bernardino, CA 92410
909-884-4084

Eaton Detroit Spring, Inc.
1555 Michigan Avenue
Detroit, MI 48216
313-963-3839
www.eatonsprings.com

Edelbrock Corporation
2700 California Street
Torrance, CA 90503
310-781-2222
www.edelbrock.com

Electromotive, Inc.
9131 Centreville Road
Manassas, VA 20110
703 331-0100
www.electromotive-inc.com

Flaming River Industries, Inc.
800 Poertner Drive
Berea, OH 44017
1-800-648-8022
www.flamingriver.com

G&J Aircraft & Competition
1115 Sultana Avenue
Ontario, CA 91761-3340
909-986-6534
www.gandjaircraft.net

Glistens Custom Metal Polishing
1441 Pomona Road, #21
Corona, CA 92882
909-734-2987

GM Performance Parts
www.gmperformanceparts.com

Goodmark Industries
625-E Old Norcross Road
Lawrenceville, GA 30045
770-339-8557 or 562-282-0284
www.goodmarkindustries.com

Hilborn Fuel Injection
22892 Glenwood Drive
Aliso Viejo, CA 92656
949-360-0909
www.hilborninjection.com

Kinsler Fuel Injection
1834 Thunderbird Street
Troy, MI 48084
248-362-1145
www.kinsler.com

Kramer Automotive Specialties
P.O. Box 5
Herman, PA 16039
724-285-5566
www.kramerauto.com

Mancini Racing
33524 Kelly Road
Clinton Township, MI 48035
800-843-2821
www.manciniracing.com

Moon Equipment
10820 S. Norwalk Boulevard
Santa Fe Springs, CA 90670
800-547-5422

OEM Paints, Inc.
Escondido, CA 92046-1736
760-747-2100
www.oempaints.com

Powermaster
7501 Strawplains Pike
Knoxville, TN 37924
800-862-7223

Schumacher Creative Services
2025 NE 123rd Street
Seattle, WA 98125
206-364-7151
www.engine-swaps.com

Summit Racing Equipment
P.O. Box 909
Akron, OH 44398-6177
800-230-3030
www.summitracing.com

Superior Automotive
2675 W. Woodland Drive
Anaheim, CA 92801
714-503-1880
www.superiorautomotive.com

Imperial Services
P.O. Box 112
Frankenmuth, MI 48734-0112
989-652-6309
www.imperialservices.net

Sutton Engineering
220 S. 9th Avenue
City of Industry, CA
626-961-9369

Total Cost Involved Engineering, Inc.
1416 W. Brooks Street
Ontario, CA 91762
800-984-6259
www.totalcostinvolved.com

Vintage Engineering
650-464-0616
www.vintageeng.com

Young Gun Performance Coatings
10611 Pullman Court
Rancho Cucamonga, CA
909-944-4156
www.youngguncoatings.com

MORE GREAT TITLES AVAILABLE FROM CARTECH®

CHEVROLET

How To Rebuild the Small-Block Chevrolet* (SA26)
Chevrolet Small-Block Parts Interchange Manual (SA55)
How To Build Max Perf Chevy Small-Blocks on a Budget (SA57)
How To Build High-Perf Chevy LS1/LS6 Engines (SA86)
How To Build Big-Inch Chevy Small-Blocks (SA87)
How to Build High-Performance Chevy Small-Block Cams/Valvetrains (SA105P)
Rebuilding the Small-Block Chevy: Step-by-Step Videobook (SA116)
High-Performance Chevy Small-Block Cylinder Heads (SA125P)
How to Rebuild the Big-Block Chevrolet* (SA142P)
How to Build Max-Performance Chevy Big Block on a Budget (SA198)
How to Restore Your Camaro 1967–1969 (SA178)
How to Build Killer Big-Block Chevy Engines (SA190)
Small-Block Chevy Performance: 1955-1996 (SA110P)
How to Build Small-Block Chevy Circle-Track Racing Engines (SA121P)
High-Performance C5 Corvette Builder's Guide (SA127P)
Chevrolet Big Block Parts Interchange Manual (SA31P)
Chevy TPI Fuel Injection Swapper's Guide (SA53P)
How to Rebuild & Modify Chevy 348/409 Engines (SA210)

FORD

High-Performance Ford Engine Parts Interchange (SA56)
How To Build Max Performance Ford V-8s on a Budget (SA69P)
How To Build Max Perf 4.6 Liter Ford Engines (SA82P)
How To Build Big-Inch Ford Small-Blocks (SA85P)
How to Rebuild the Small-Block Ford* (SA102)
How to Rebuild Big-Block Ford Engines* (SA162P)
Full-Size Fords 1955–1970 (SA176P)
How to Build Max-Performance Ford FE Engines (SA183)
How to Restore Your Mustang 1964 1/2–1973 (SA165)
How to Build Ford RestoMod Street Machines (SA101P)
Building 4.6/5.4L Ford Horsepower on the Dyno (SA115P)
How to Rebuild 4.6/5.4-Liter Ford Engines* (SA155P)
Building High-Performance Fox-Body Mustangs on a Budget (SA75P)
How to Build Supercharged & Turbocharged Small-Block Fords (SA95P)
How to Rebuild & Modify Ford C4 & C6 Automatic Transmissions (SA227)
How to Rebuild Ford Power Stroke Diesel (SA213)

GENERAL MOTORS

GM Automatic Overdrive Transmission Builder's and Swapper's Guide (SA140)
How to Rebuild GM LS-Series Engines* (SA147)
How to Swap GM LS-Series Engines Into Almost Anything (SA156)
How to Supercharge & Turbocharge GM LS-Series Engines (SA180)
How to Build Big-Inch GM LS-Series Engines (SA203)
How to Rebuild & Modify GM Turbo 400 Transmissions* (SA186)
How to Build GM Pro-Touring Street Machines (SA81P)

MOPAR

How to Rebuild the Big-Block Mopar* (SA197)
How to Rebuild the Small-Block Mopar* (SA143P)
How to Build Max-Performance Hemi Engines (SA164P)
How To Build Max-Performance Mopar Big Blocks (SA171P)
Mopar B-Body Performance Upgrades 1962-1979 (SA191)
How to Build Big-Inch Mopar Small-Blocks (SA104P)
High-Performance New Hemi Builder's Guide 2003-Present (SA132P)

OLDSMOBILE/ PONTIAC/ BUICK

How to Build Max-Performance Oldsmobile V-8s (SA172P)
How To Build Max-Perf Pontiac V-8s (SA78)
How to Rebuild Pontiac V-8s* (SA200)
How to Build Max-Performance Buick Engines (SA146P)

SPORT COMPACTS

Honda Engine Swaps (SA93P)
High-Performance Subaru Builder's Guide (SA141)
How to Build Max-Performance Mitsubishi 4G63t Engines (SA148P)
How to Rebuild Honda B-Series Engines* (SA154)
The New Mini Performance Handbook (SA182P)
High Performance Dodge Neon Builder's Handbook (SA100P)
High-Performance Honda Builder's Handbook Volume 1 (SA49P)
How to Build Cobra Kit Cars + Buying Used (SA202)

*Workbench® Series books feature step-by-step instruction with hundreds of color photos for stock rebuilds and automotive repair.

ENGINE

Engine Blueprinting (SA21)
Automotive Diagnostic Systems: Understanding OBD-I & OBD II (SA174)
Competition Engine Building (SA214)

INDUCTION & IGNITION

Super Tuning & Modifying Holley Carburetors (SA08)
Street Supercharging, A Complete Guide to (SA17)
How To Build High-Performance Ignition Systems (SA79P)
How to Build and Modify Rochester Quadrajet Carburetors (SA113)
Turbo: Real World High-Performance Turbocharger Systems (SA123)
How to Rebuild & Modify Carter/Edelbrock Carbs (SA130P)
Engine Management: Advanced Tuning (SA135)
Designing & Tuning High-Performance Fuel Injection Systems (SA161)
Demon Carburetion (SA68P)

DRIVING

How to Drift: The Art of Oversteer (SA118P)
How to Drag Race (SA136P)
How to Autocross (SA158P)
How to Hook and Launch (SA195)

HIGH-PERFORMANCE & RESTORATION HOW-TO

How To Install and Tune Nitrous Oxide Systems (SA194)
David Vizard's How to Build Horsepower (SA24)
How to Rebuild & Modify High-Performance Manual Transmissions* (SA103)
High-Performance Jeep Cherokee XJ Builder's Guide 1984–2001 (SA109P)
How to Paint Your Car on a Budget (SA117)
High Performance Brake Systems (SA126P)
High Performance Diesel Builder's Guide (SA129P)
4x4 Suspension Handbook (SA137)
Automotive Welding: A Practical Guide* (SA159)
Automotive Wiring and Electrical Systems* (SA160)
Design & Install In-Car Entertainment Systems (SA163P)
Automotive Bodywork & Rust Repair* (SA166)
High-Performance Differentials, Axles, & Drivelines (SA170)
How to Make Your Muscle Car Handle (SA175)
Rebuilding Any Automotive Engine: Step-by-Step Videobook (SA179)
Builder's Guide to Hot Rod Chassis & Suspension (SA185)
How To Rebuild & Modify GM Turbo 400 Transmissions* (SA186)
How to Build Altered Wheelbase Cars (SA189P)
How to Build Period Correct Hot Rods (SA192)
Automotive Sheet Metal Forming & Fabrication (SA196)
Performance Automotive Engine Math (SA204)
How to Design, Build & Equip Your Automotive Workshop on a Budget (SA207)
Automotive Electrical Performance Projects (SA209)
How to Port & Flow Test Cylinder Heads (SA215)
High Performance Jeep Wrangler TJ Builder's Guide: 1997-2006 (SA120P)
Dyno Testing & Tuning (SA138P)
How to Rebuild Any Automotive Engine (SA151P)
Muscle Car Interior Restoration Guide (SA167P)
How to Build Horsepower - Volume 2 (SA52P)
Advanced Automotive Welding (SA235)
How to Restore Your Corvette (SA223)
How to Restore Your Pontiac GTO (SA218)

HISTORIES & PERSONALITIES

Yenko (CT485)
Lost Hot Rods (CT487)
Lost Hot Rods II (CT506)
Grumpy's Toys (CT489)
America's Coolest Station Wagons (CT493)
Super Stock — A paperback version of a classic best seller. (CT495)
Rusty Pickups: American Workhorses Put to Pasture (CT496)
Jerry Heasley's Rare Finds — Great collection of Heasley's best finds. (CT497)
Jerry Heasley's Rare Finds: Mustangs & Fords (CT509)
Street Sleepers: The Art of the Deceptively Fast Car (CT498)
Rat Rods: Rodding's Imperfect Stepchildren (CT486)
East vs. West Showdown: Rods, Customs Rails (CT501)
Junior Stock: Stock Class Drag Racing 1964–1971 (CT505)
Definitive Shelby Mustang Guide 1965–1970, The (CT507)
Hurst Equipped (CT490)

CarTech®, Inc. 39966 Grand Ave., North Branch, MN 55056. Ph: 800-551-4754 or 651-277-1200 • Fax: 651-277-1203
Brooklands Books Ltd., PO Box 146 Cobham, Surrey KT11 1LG, England. Ph: 01932 865051 • Fax 01932 868803
Brooklands Books Aus., 3/37-39 Green Street, Banksmeadow, NSW 2019, Australia. Ph: 2 9695 7055 • Fax 2 9695 7355

Visit us online at
www.cartechbooks.com for more info!

Additional books that may interest you...

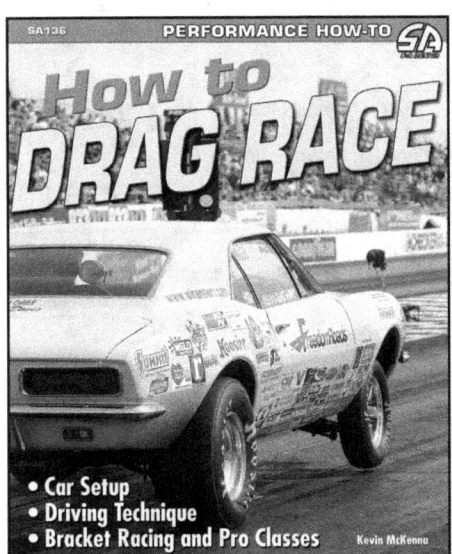

HOW TO DRAG RACE by Kevin McKenna Author Kevin McKenna, senior editor at *National DRAGSTER*, NHRA's weekly news magazine, uses 300 color photos to show you what to expect your first time out, how to set up your street car or race car for consistency and speed, and driving techniques for racers at all levels. He discusses tires, safety equipment, driving aids such as line-locks and delay boxes, choosing a class, and advanced racer math. Special sections detail how to maximize your setup and strategy for bracket racing success. If you have ever thought it would be fun to give drag racing a try, this book is for you. Softbound, 8.5 x 11 inches, 144 pages, 300 color photos. *Item # SA136*

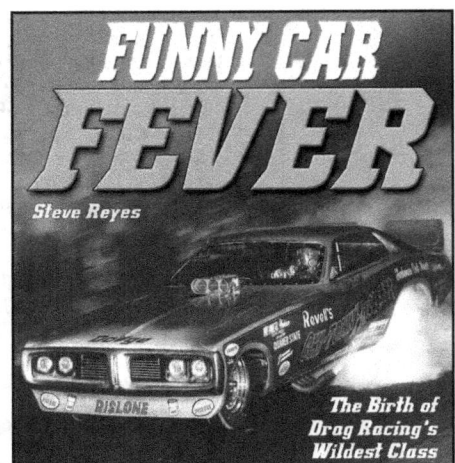

FUNNY CAR FEVER by Steve Reyes There wasn't always a class for these "funny-looking" cars. In the mid 60s, many of drag racing's fastest drivers were outgrowing the Super Stock and Factory Experimental classes, building cars that stretched and eventually broke the rules. Promoters discovered they could pair up these altered-wheelbase, injected, blown machines in exhibition match races—and the spectators came running. This is a humorous, heart-felt, first-hand account of the most exciting and memorable years of the Funny Car class, and it includes over 350 of Reyes' favorite images and never-before-heard stories to bring the feeling of the class and the era home to you. Softbound, 9 x 9 inches, 192 pages, 200 color & 150 b/w photos. *Item # CT443*

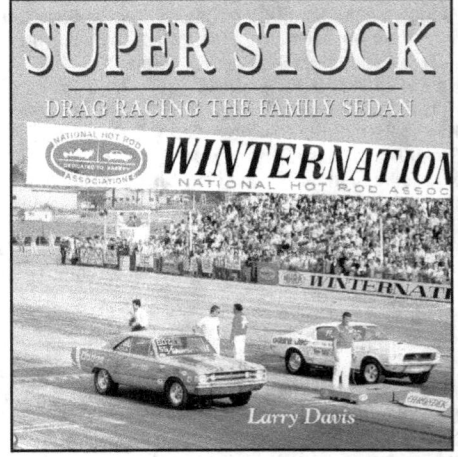

SUPER STOCK: Drag Racing the Family Sedan by Larry Davis This book traces the evolution of the cars, the engines, the rules, the personalities, and many of the teams, from its beginnings in the mid 50s through to the 60s and the era of the Super Stock 409s, Ramchargers, 421 Pontiacs, and 406 Fords. This was a time when Ford, Chrysler, and General Motors competed on a weekly basis at local drag strips throughout the country, and the saying "Win on Sunday, sell on Monday" had real significance in the marketplace. The hardcover best seller is gone, but now you can get it in paperback. Softbound, 9 x 9 inches, 210 pages, 310 color & b/w photos. *Item # CT495*

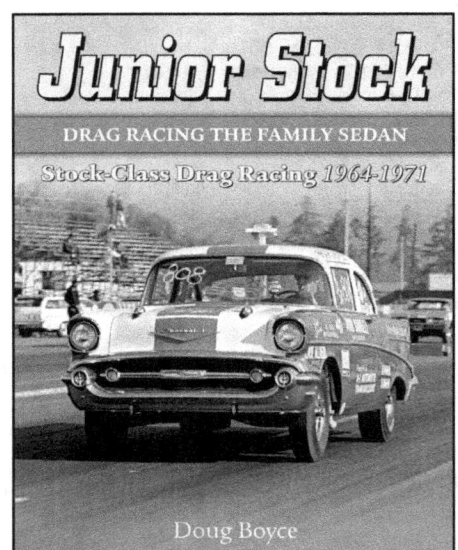

JUNIOR STOCK: Drag Racing the Family Sedan by Doug Boyce In the 1950s and 1960s, drag racing was an exciting new sport that anyone with a car could participate in. Based on their equipment, the participants' cars were assigned to specific classes. This class format encouraged amateur participation on a level never before seen. Drag racing was a popular hobby for many, and their competition vehicles were typically street cars that had been strategically upgraded to the limits of their specific class. The end of the class structure meant a great loss in the sport's popularity, but these amazing times will never be forgotten. Stock-class drag racing is celebrated in this new book, with hundreds of vintage color photographs showing the way it used to be. Softbound, 8.5 x 11 inches, 176 pages, 450 color photos. *Item # CT505*

Check out our new website:
CarTechBooks.com

✓ Find our newest books before anyone else

✓ Get weekly tech tips from our experts

✓ Get your ride or project featured on our homepage!

**Exclusive Promotions and Giveaways on Facebook
Like us to WIN! Facebook.com/CarTechBooks**

www.cartechbooks.com or 1-800-551-4754

www.ingramcontent.com/pod-product-compliance
Lightning Source LLC
Chambersburg PA
CBHW051412070526
44584CB00023B/3397